SUPERNATURAL ISLE OF MAN

Jenny Randles has been a prolific investigator into the unexplained for more than 25 years. Her books have appeared in 28 countries and have sold well over one million copies. Her previous titles include *Beyond Explanation?, Abduction, Sixth Sense, Phantoms of the Soap Operas, Crop Circles: A Mystery Solved (with Paul Fuller), The Paranormal Year, Spontaneous Human Combustion* (with Peter Hough), *Aliens: The Real Story, Star Children, Something in the Air* and *Supernatural Pennines* – all published by Hale. Jenny has appeared many times on TV and radio and has written and presented her own programmes about the supernatural for the BBC and IBA. She was story consultant to the hit ITV series *Strange But True?* Born in the Pennines, Jenny now lives in North Wales. She has visited the Isle of Man many times and fell under its spell as a young child.

by Jenny Randles

Beyond Explanation?
Abduction
Sixth Sense
Phantoms of the Soap Operas
The Paranormal Year: 1993 Edition
Aliens: The Real Story
Star Children
Something in the Air
Supernatural Pennines

With Paul Fuller

Crop Circles: A Mystery Solved

With Peter Hough

Spontaneous Human Combustion

SUPERNATURAL ISLE *of* MAN

JENNY RANDLES

Edited by Sue Woolley

www.lilypublications.co.uk

First published in Great Britain 2003
Paperback edition 2006 (Robert Hale Limited)

ISBN 978-1-907945-68-7

A catalogue record for this book is available from the British Library

Contents

Illustrations

Page:

Foreword

Ellan Vannin, as the Isle of Man is poetically named in Manx Gaelic, is quite possibly my favourite spot on earth. I have visited its shores often since my first visit at the age of eight, and it has changed little over the years. I suspect that this book might display some of my affection for this land – an affection it seems to evoke in most of its regular visitors.

The Isle of Man is a delicious hybrid of the familiar and the unfamiliar; a place which is sufficiently 'weird' that it allows one to feel as if one has found a whole new country that somehow escaped mention on any atlas – a destination that can only be reached by time machine.

The Island feels slightly 'supernatural' simply because it is such a pleasantly odd place to be. Indeed, there is probably no other place where the weird and the mystical remain so close to the community; where many of the Celtic myths, legends and traditions are still recognized and the influence of the *fairies, bugganes* and other supernatural creatures is as strong as ever in some parts.

Of course, the Island is not simply about traditions and fairy beliefs: it also has its own share of modern mysteries, from UFOs to poltergeists. We will naturally be looking in detail at some of these.

Because the Isle of Man is so easy to reach and simple to get around I have designed the text in the format of a guidebook. This should bring home the sense of oddity that is as infused into the landscape as morning dew is upon the grass.

Some facts about the Isle of Man:

The Isle of Man, otherwise known as Mann or Mannin, is a self-governing British Crown Dependency, located in the Irish Sea between between England, Scotland, Wales and Northern Ireland. The head of state is the Queen, who holds the title of Lord of Mann and is represented by a Lieutenant Governor.

The Island has been inhabited since before 6,500 BC. Megalithic monuments such as those at Cashtal yn Ard in the parish of Maughold, King Orry's Grave at Laxey, Meayll Circle near Cregneash, and Ballaharra Stones at St John's date from this era.

Gaelic cultural influence began in the 5th century AD, and the Manx language, a branch of the Gaelic languages, gradually emerged.

The Vikings arrived in the 9th century and inter-married with the Manx. This gave rise to a Norse-Gaelic culture that is reflected in many place-names.

Godred Crovan (known by the Manx as King Orry), ruled as King of Mann and the Isles from 1079 – 1095. He established peace and introduced the Norse system of government, Tynwald, which endures to this day and is said to be the world's oldest continuous parliament. He is immortalised in the National Anthem, 'O Land of Our Birth'.

In 1266, the Island came under Scottish rule. A period of alternating rule by the kings of Scotland and England followed. The Island came under the feudal lordship of the English Crown in 1399. The lordship revested into the British Crown in 1765, but the Island retains its status as an internally self-governing Crown Dependency.

The Isle of Man is 52 kilometres (32 miles) long and, at its widest point, 22 kilometres (14 miles) wide. It has an area of around 572 square kilometres (221 sq miles). It has a total of 688 miles (1,107 km) of public roads. In addition, it has a unique vintage transport system of narrow-gauge steam railway and an electric railway.

Snaefell (Norse for Snow Mountain), with a height of 621 metres (2,037 ft) is the highest peak. According to an old saying, from the summit one can see six kingdoms: those of Mann, Scotland, England, Ireland, Wales – and Heaven. Some versions add a seventh, the Sea.

1
Themselves: The Supernatural Entities of the Isle of Man

At this point it is appropriate to introduce you to the cast of characters, for the Isle of Man has its own breed of strange beings. As these names appear in the pages that follow this is the best place to tell you a little about each of them. Then we can set off on our tour, to meet them in their supernatural habitat. Key references to locations throughout the text are given in brackets to provide an Ordnance Survey reference to facilitate your investigations. These relate to the OS map 95 (Isle of Man), which is available from bookstores or libraries.

First, a general warning is needed: collectively in Celtic nations, and certainly on this Isle of Man, it is regarded as ill-mannered to refer to these beings as Fairies. Instead, they are called the 'Little People', or the 'Lil' Boys', or commonly, 'Themselves'.

Besides the Little People, there are other alarming folk. Here, in alphabetical order, are some of those creatures.

Ben varrey

Being an island, it is no surprise that Mann is one of the hotspots for mer-folk in the northern hemisphere. The *ben varrey* (Mx. Gaelic, woman of the sea) is the Manx mermaid. More like a siren than an evil temptress, this half-woman, half-fish creature frequents rocks by the shore. She loves the company of fishermen and courts their friendship with amorous smiles and kind gestures, bestowing good fortune and rarely inflicting harm, unless mistreated.

Sightings have been common in the south and east. Off Langness (SC 276 652) there are stories of a submerged city inhabited by mer-folk. Some more recent reports, especially those from around Spanish Head (SC 180 659), speak of 'smooth-skinned beings' sitting on rocks, behaving with remarkable intelligence. But as there is a healthy seal population in this area it is tempting to suspect this may be the origin of such legends.

Buggane

This is the Manx equivalent of the *bogey-man* (this popular phrase itself being a derivation of the old name for a goblin-like creature found in many parts of the British Isles, including the Lancashire *boggart*). *Bugganes* are said to be monstrous wild men with an ability to change size and shape at will in order to terrify people and lay claim to a place. They make roaring noises and have been known to throw heavy objects – including rocks – and chase and capture anyone who invades their territory.

Perhaps the most notorious is the *buggane* who lived on Greeba Mountain (SC 317 816), Marown. His fierce presence is said to have prevented the completion of St Trinian's Church, the roofless ruins of which are still clearly visible from the busy Peel to Douglas road.

There is another account of a *buggane*, in the form of a wild, hairy man, with pointed ears and eyes like fire, at Spooyt Vooar waterfall, Glen Maye (SC 232 798).

Dooinney-oie

The *dooinney-oie* (Mx. Gaelic, night man) is a demon not unlike the Irish *banshee*, who predicts an imminent death by incessant wailing. The *dooinney-oie* is a little less fearsome. More commonly, he was simply heard, not seen, uttering a howl that resembled the playing of a loud horn. When the *dooinney-oie* was heard, locals believed that storms were due and it was a signal to batten down the hatches.

The *dooinney-oie* is most commonly associated with rocky places, caves and inlets around Laxey and his legend may owe its origin to the sound made by the wind shifting as bad weather sets in, causing echoing noises when the sea lashes against the rocks. 'How-laa' is his spectral cry!

Fynoderee

No matter how his name is spelt ('phynnodderee' is also common), this creature is one of the Island's most celebrated entities. The last was reported to be living, in exile, atop the Island's second highest hill, North Barrule (SC 442 909).

Variously described as a satyr, (half-human, half-beast) or a brownie (a small, man-sized elf noted for being a hard-working friend to country folk), tradition has it that the *fynoderee* (Mx Gaelic 'hairyone) originated in Glen Auldyn, near Ramsey, where he fell in love with a woman and, as a consequence, was banished from his own realm to live amongst humans. Once of fair appearance, he was given the form of a hairy man with red eyes and a swarthy complexion as further punishment for having disobeyed the rules.

The *fynoderee* was noted for his prodigious strength and would assist farmers, especially with the mowing of their fields. He would become rather upset, however, if his handiwork was criticized.

Glashtin

The *glashtin* or *glashtyn* (Mx. Gaelic, water-horse) is recalled in very ancient tales and usually then with such words as, 'In the olden days there used to be . . .', implying they have long-since disappeared. They may indeed be a memory of an actual race that pre-dated the Celts, passed on from generation to generation. They are described as strong and able to shape-shift, preferring isolation to the company of people, but, like the *fynoderee*, willing to help out on the farms, particularly with the livestock.

Lhiannan-shee

The *lhiannan-she* (Mx. Gaelic, spirit friend) was a sort of female 'demon lover' who attached herself in amorous ways to human men. In form, she closely resemble a succubus – an entity reported all over the world since records began (although today they are usually given tabloid-inspired names such as 'randy ghost' or 'bed-hopping phantom'!).

Another name ascribed to this class of entity since ancient times is 'night mare' meaning 'woman of the night'. We, of course, have adopted the same term to mean something rather different – a frightening dream that disturbs us in the wee small hours. But its derivation is from much more supernatural origins.

Encounters usually involve the female demon attaching herself to a lover or his bed and courting him forcibly. Modern investigations centre on tales of paralysis and a sense of presence during these amorous advances, but rarely any clear visible sign of a demon. It is believed by some scientists that these accounts stem from what is called 'sleep paralysis', a natural process that we all undergo during dreaming-sleep, but of which we have no conscious awareness. In rare cases a person can become conscious during this paralysis and inevitably feel that they are under some sort of frightening assault. In many modern reports, the bedroom visitor is interpreted not as a demon but as an alien preparing to abduct them; yet such reports are largely indistinguishable from encounters with the *lhiannan-shee*.

Moddey Dhoo

The moddey dhoo (Mx. Gaelic, black dog) is also the equivalent of another entity widely reported beyond the Island. There have been sightings of this large, black-coated animal with flashing red eyes across the British Isles. In the Isle of Man, its most famous incarnation is in connection with Peel Castle (SC 241 845). Indeed the story was sufficiently famous to have been written about by Sir Walter Scott.

When it appears, the *moddey dhoo* is supposed to act as a guardian. For example, it has been known to prevent fishermen from sailing before the weather turned, which might otherwise have led to their deaths. But it is also considered wise not to mock or cross it, as those who do so may suffer dire consequences – if only as a result of the terror it inspires when seen disappearing through walls!

Modern sightings tend to be subsumed into the category known these days as ABCs (Alien Big Cats), in which large, black animals, commonly taken for pumas or dogs, stalk wild moors and then vanish without trace. Arguments rage as to whether these are misperceptions of stray dogs, reports of unusually large but native wild cats or are real big cats (such as lynx) that once inhabited these islands and have survived in isolated pockets or even been released into the countryside by zoo owners.

However, their supernatural behaviour and the near total lack of physical evidence (carcasses are rarely, if ever, discovered) makes their comparison with the *moddey dhoo* seem more obvious.

Tarroo-ushtey

The *tarroo-ushtey* (Mx. Gaelic, water bull), is said to be a demon bull with a fondness for water and for pulling tricks. When seen, it appears just like a normal bull but defies capture. Farmers who tried to subdue the creature, paid the price, either with poor harvests or by being carried off towards the river. In one case, a man barely escaped with his life as the bull leapt into the water.

Encounters with the *tarroo-ushtey* as a dark shambling form seen crossing the roadway at night remind one of many early land sightings of the Loch Ness monster.

In Mann, it is likely that, with the *tarroo-ushtey* legend so firmly in mind, any mysterious large animal vaguely seen at night would have been considered a candidate for the supernatural bull. This is particularly so in the region of Glen Maye, where the *tarroo-ushtey* was widely feared – and where so many other strange phenomena have been reported.

2
Early Manx Mythology

The stories that follow describe the creation and nature of the Isle of Man and are part of the mythology that centre on its possession of supernatural power. Of course they are legends, as opposed to proven fact, but all are ancient tales, many dating back at least 1,000 years, or even older. The unusual creation myths support the view that the Manx live in a supernaturally-blessed location.

A New Land

There are two versions of the story of the birth of the Isle of Man, often referred to simply as 'Mann'. One is mythical, the other pseudo-historical.

According to mythology Mann owes its creation to the Irish giant Finn MacCooil, who was engaged in a battle against a rival Scottish giant. Following a noisy confrontation, the Scottish giant went scurrying back across the Irish Sea. In a desperate move to defeat him, Finn scooped up a mass of rock from the ground and threw it at his fleeing assailant. He missed and the rock fell short into the midst of the ocean where it became the Isle of Man. The hole left behind in Ireland was a huge scar that filled with water and is now known as Lough Neagh.

As the years passed, rising water levels caused parts of the Manx coastline to disappear under the ocean and only the tops remained visible as jagged rocks, especially around the Calf of Man, the small island off the southern tip of the main Island.

The pseudo-historical version is not so different in essence from this legend and has been passed down by oral tradition from both ancient Irish and Manx sources:

There were scattered tribes in Ireland in those far distant days, each fearful of invasion by marauders from across the sea, so they banded together to face this onslaught, but soon fell into civil war.

Suddenly the sky turned dark and the sunlight vanished as a great roaring noise filled the air and the ground began to tremble. When light returned and the shaking ceased, not only were some of the tribesmen lost without trace, but so was part of the land, where a huge scar had appeared. The sea was left in a state of great agitation after this tragedy, with waves unlike any seen before. Mariners caught out in their boats during the catastrophe had to cling on tightly to save themselves from drowning.

After the waters returned to normal and fishermen began to venture eastwards again, a new land mass was seen to have appeared where none had been visible before. They called it 'Mann' after the sea-god, Manannan.

These different versions do have elements in common and the latter, to modern scientific ears, is curiously suggestive of something that might actually have taken place. A huge shadow passes over the earth, the sun is blocked out, the ground shakes, there is a roaring sound, the land is left scarred and tidal waves appear. All this resembles the predictable aftermath of a great earthquake. But earthquakes of this magnitude would only occur in the British Isles if something amazing had triggered them. The giant shadow may thus be the potential cause

– a meteorite impact that struck somewhere in northern Europe, causing geological upheaval and blotting out the sun with debris cast into the atmosphere.

There are a number of ancient records describing similar catastrophes (including biblical references and Greek and Roman texts), and some scholars believe they may relate to old folk memories of an actual disaster that occurred at the dawn of modern human habitation – perhaps 10,000 years ago.

Only since the 1990s has it become known that large meteorites strike the earth with a greater frequency than was previously believed. A major impact in Siberia occurred in June 1908 and, with the force of an atom bomb, destroyed hundreds of square miles of tundra. Even larger impacts are believed to have occurred on earth every few thousand years. Their tell-tale remains can be traced by modern satellite photography, which can find impact craters otherwise lost deep under the ocean.

Several modest impacts are believed to have occurred in Europe in ancient times and at least one is likely to have been of sufficient size to cause obvious – if short-term – events that would be powerful enough to inspire legends. These tales would inevitably be retold around the camp fire from generation to generation, resulting perhaps in this Manx creation myth.

Any sufficiently large meteorite impact, even hundreds of miles from the Irish coast, would have devastating consequences for the local tribes and could have been like those described in these old tales. There would be earthquakes of the order never seen before. The sky would turn dark. And if the impact came in the ocean then tidal waves would be inevitable.

Geologically it is most unlikely that such an act of nature could have raised the Isle of Man from beneath the waves, but it may be that, had the Island not been discovered before the impact, its aftermath likely forced these early Celtic tribes to exploit fishing more than before. The darkening skies and atmospheric disruption could have led to several years of bitter weather and decades of crop failure. If the tribes ventured further east in search of fish and discovered Mann for the first time, its presence in the Irish Sea might well have seemed to be connected. Did it become linked with the meteor impact in an understandable, though false, cause and effect?

For a meteor passing above, read the hand of a legendary giant in the mind of naïve people. A boulder of rock crashing into the ocean is perhaps not a bad description of a meteor strike. It may be that the discovery of the Island was the result of a celestial event that inspired tales that have lived on for thousands of years and which, only now, can we understand.

The Mist

If you arrive by sea, the Island can seem to emerge rather suddenly out of the water, protected by a curtain of mist. This is a natural feature caused by the presence of a large landmass amidst a cold ocean, which preserves an oasis of milder weather within less temperate surroundings.

However, this curtain has long been regarded as a supernatural attribute of the Island, placed there to make it invisible to passing ships. And this mist is connected with the Island name itself. Mann was, certainly from its first discovery until around 800 AD, considered Irish territory. Indeed there are stories about another Finn, not a mythical giant but an actual merchant or pirate from around 150 AD. The tales of his exploits whilst passing to and from this barely inhabited island further imbue it with a clear sense of it being a province of Ireland.

Although *Ellan Sheaynt* (Isle of Tranquillity), as it was originally known, was well off the beaten track, the ancient inhabitants of Ireland regarded it as being under the watchful eye of a great magician named Manannan Mac Lir (Manannan, Son of the Sea).

Manannan was a member of an ancient mystic Irish ruling race, the Tuatha de Dannan, widely considered by folklorists to have been the original beings that are now celebrated as the fairy folk often referred to in the Isle of Man as 'Themselves'). The Tuatha had supernatural abilities and lived inside hollow hills where time lost all meaning. This allowed them to live apart from mortals, who increasingly dreaded their presence and eventually drove them into permanent hiding.

Over the years, as Christianity spread slowly across the region, these beings were subjected to demystification and became relegated first to the status of cheap wizards and then to pagan merchants. Manannan is, therefore, variously described as either the Celtic god of the sea, who protected Ellan Vannin, or a magician who used the Island as a sort of rest home for other mystics after they were driven out of Ireland. Later still, he became a skilled navigator who used the Island as a trading link between Ireland and Britain.

There are linguistic disputes over whether the name for the Island is derived directly from the Manannan, but the sea-god and the Isle of Man are certainly linked. Annan, a town in Dumfries and Galloway (on the region of the Scottish mainland closest to the Island), seems to have similar origins. Manannan ended his days in Scotland and also spent time in Wales, where the great mystic text the Mabinogian refers to a similar magical figure who ruled the Irish Sea.

To what extent these records are independent or merely borrow from the same basic legend is impossible to judge so many centuries later, but references to this mystic entity are still widespread: the mist that surrounds the Island and makes it invisible is often called Manannan's Cloak, and the thrilling interactive history centre in Peel is named 'House of Manannan'.

Tir Na Nog

Manannan crossed his domain, the sea, in a supernatural vehicle called 'Wave Sweeper', which glided across the waters without visible means of power. He surveyed the waters westwards towards a mystical land of Tir Na Nog. It is not clear how closely this should be associated with the Isle of Man, as its true origin (if the island ever existed outside of mythology) is uncertain. Most sources think that it was further into the Atlantic. But perhaps it was not.

Tir Na Nog is also known as the Island of Eternal Youth. Interestingly, it was said to be magically protected from human eyes. With an equitable climate it was a source of refuge to which the last members of the Tuatha de Dannan fled after being driven from Ireland. So supernaturally empowered was Tir Na Nog that time stood still there and its inhabitants did not experience ageing as they would elsewhere. For this reason humans were rarely allowed to visit and when they did so they were frequently 'enchanted' to prevent them from recalling its location, so that they could not return.

One story is told in Scottish folklore of a human who visited Tir Na Nog. Tiernan Farrell, a fisherman from Arran, was met by a strange being on the quayside after a fishing expedition. It was a tall man with flaming hair, who asked if Farrell could transport cargo between the islands. He confirmed that he could. The stranger loaded barrels of meat on to his ship and they set sail south-westwards, beyond the waters in which he would normally fish.

Growing concerned as they sailed away from any land that he knew, Farrell asked the strange man if he was sure of his destination. 'Yes,' he was told. But fear compounded itself even further when a strange cloak of mist suddenly covered the Irish Sea and they sailed on without any reference point to guide them.

Forty-eight hours after sailing in this mist, the skies suddenly cleared and the tiny fishing boat arrived at the shore of a green land that reared up out of the waters as if from nowhere. Stepping ashore, Farrell said to his passenger, 'Tir Na Nog – but I thought it was a myth.' The flame-haired man merely smiled and assured him that he was indeed an inhabitant of this blessed place.

As soon as Farrell stepped ashore he felt rejuvenated by the aura of this magical island. The years had melted away. He told the stranger that he wished to stay, but this did not meet with his approval. However, he was invited to have a drink before they unloaded the meat and he was given a strange, sweet-tasting, amber liquid, poured from a sack. But as soon as he drank he began to grow tired, and his next memory was of waking, alone in his boat, drifting back towards Arran with no sign of his passenger or the mysterious island. There was, however, a large sack on the floor of his boat that had not been there before.

Despite feeling old and tired once more, and deeply saddened that he had lost the chance to live in the land of eternal youth, Farrell did at least have some compensation. When he opened the sack it was loaded with coins and jewels. 'If I cannot be young then at least I can be rich,' he said to himself philosophically. Despite trying often, he never found Tir Na Nog again.

Tir Na Nog and the Isle of Man clearly share some similarities. Such stories in the Celtic psyche certainly helped to ensure that the Island's association with the supernatural was firmly established. Moreover, anyone who has ever read modern accounts of alleged alien abductions will notice vivid comparisons popping up here.

In these cases, recorded in their thousands over the past fifty years (see my book Abduction), a person often describes seeing a strange figure much like the man on the Arran quayside. They enter a peculiar structure surrounded by mist that they assume to be an alien craft, go on to have a weird conversation and then find themselves losing all sense of the passage of time. Not infrequently they suddenly 'come to' back on the road that they were originally travelling, with all trace of the strange man having vanished. In a significant number of these space-age encounters, the abductee is even given a peculiar liquid to drink, which seems to precipitate loss of consciousness and return them to normality. Very few of these witnesses are aware of the legend of Tir Na Nog or that they have just described a modern version of a very ancient tale.

Three Legs of Man

Utterly synonymous with the Isle of Man is the Three Legs of Man symbol. It is found the nation's flag, its coins, stamps and public buildings. The Three Legs is a peculiar image, quite literally three legs joined together in the form of a wheel or circle. The legs appear to be rotating, although in which direction they are moving has been the source of endless discussion. Clockwise is the officially decreed answer to prevent further argument!

The Three Legs is the very symbol of independence by which Mann thrives. Since medieval times it has been associated with the Island's motto, *Quocunque Jeceris Stabit* (Latin, 'Whichever Way I am Thrown

I Will Stand'). but its origins go back much further.

According to ancient myth, Manannan threw a magical silvery-blue mantle round the Island to make it invisible to passing ships and so safe from invasion. Up until some 2,500 years ago this ruse was said to have been largely successful, the mist being maintained by an eternal fire. However, a group of fishermen were driven through the mist during a terrible storm and were saved only because they were thrown up onto the shores of the Island. Once safe they sought to light a fire to recover from their terrible ordeal, but as they used their tinder box a huge noise emerged from the dark cloud that enshrouded the land.

A strange object appeared in the shape of three legs joined together like the spokes of a wheel. The apparition began to revolve and moved with the cloud up the sides of the hills above the shore, while the fishermen watched in awe.

This story is remarkably like a very old UFO encounter. There have, in fact, been many modern sightings of UFOs shaped like revolving wheels, and it is by no means unusual for such objects to be surrounded by a curtain of silvery-blue mist. Indeed, there is little doubt that if this incident was being described today, the symbol of the Isle of Man would be regarded as a flying saucer!

Legend has it that Manannan could change himself into the three-legged flying machine that emerged from the cloud as a means to terrify any who got past his barrier of mist. There are other tales of how he created an illusion that whole armies of three-legged men were wheeling about on the hilltops ready to defend the land.

Whilst, as a legend, it scarcely matters whether the presumably apocryphal three-legged wheel might have been of natural or supernatural origin, we might be tempted to consider interpreting it in more objective terms today; for the key to this story could perhaps lie in the stormy weather that forced those mariners ashore. There is a strange natural phenomenon that appears sometimes during storms known as ball lightning. Even today ball lightning is barely understood by atmospheric physicists and in days gone by its sudden and unnerving appearance was frequently associated with the supernatural.

Ball lightning often appears in the form of a rolling ball of fire that emerges out of cloud and can float, whilst still rotating, even vertically up walls and hillsides. It has been reported in a number of scientifically documented cases as possessing spokes like a wheel. Was the sighting of a wheel that inspired the symbol of the Island really a chance encounter with the power of ball lightning?

3
The History of Mann

In order to put the mystical legends about the Isle of Man into context it is a good idea to look at what we know about the history of the Island from actual evidence and archaeology. In the process I will introduce some of the sites where it is still possible to see such evidence preserved in the landscape. For like all old kingdoms, Mann has its ancient mystical structures.

The Stone Age

The first people who settled in the Isle of Man were Neolithic herdsmen and early farmers who arrived about 2,500 BC. Flint arrowheads, stone implements and fragments of from this era have been discovered around the seacoast and shores of ancient fresh-water lakes. The outline of long barrows, where they buried the dead, is part of the upland landscape. Flints and pottery fragments can be seen at the Manx Museum in Douglas.

These early settlers built megaliths such as those at Cashtal yn Ard, near Glen Mona in the parish of Maughold (SC 462 892), which was excavated in the 1930s. It consisted of a small burial chamber protected by modestly sized standing stones.

An even larger megalithic site is situated close to the main road at Laxey.

This site is known as King Orry's Grave (SC 438 843), but the name is a little misleading since it has nothing to do with this later figure who dates from the Viking era. Unfortunately, a road was cut through this particular site in more recent times, before its importance was recognized.

The Bronze Age

Between 1800 – 1700 BC, the Isle of Man saw people originally from the Continent moving into the islands of Britain. They brought with them different types of pottery and used their metal-working skills to make more sophisticated weaponry.

The large communal tombs of the Megalithic period were replaced by smaller mounds, examples of which can be seen scattered about the Manx countryside.

The Iron Age

Next to arrive (500 BC-500 AD) were the Celts, a race of people originally from central Europe who spread across mainland Britain and then to its extremities, bringing with them a knowledge of working with iron. They took action to protect the Island from invasion by building large hill forts and smaller promontory forts on coastal cliffs.

The Celts enjoyed long periods of calm and stability, especially when the Romans were in control of mainland Britain and their rule allayed the Manx fear of invasion by the unruly British. There is little sign that the Romans ever tried to subdue the Isle of Man or spent much time there.

During long periods of peace, the Celts constructed large roundhouse homesteads (some as large as 90ft. in diameter and 6,000sq.ft. in area), where families lived and space was set aside for storing grain, stabling livestock and for occupations such as spinning and weaving. Archaeological traces can be seen at Braaid Circle (SC325 765), Balladoole (SC246 682), near Castletown and Broogh Fort, Santon (SC317 742). There is a superb scale model in the Manx Museum.

They prepared themselves against possible invasion by building forts on hill tops such as Cronk Sumark, Sulby (SC 392 941) and smaller promontory forts on coastal cliffs such as Cronk ny Merriu (SC 317 704) and Burro Ned (SC 176 665), a short walk from The Sound visitors' centre.

Arrival of Christianity

It is thought that Christianity arrived on the Island from Ireland in about 450–500 AD. Tradition has it that St Patrick converted the pagan Manx to the new religion. Certainly there are many marvelous tales of how the saint landed on Inis Patrick (later site of Peel Castle) and banished the great wizard Manannan.

For several hundred years Christianity slowly merged with the old 'pagan' ways of the Celts, which have never entirely died out.

The early Christians built some 200 small chapels (keeills) all over the Island, often in very remote locations. Many ruins can be easily seen today.

Among the Irish saints who, in legend, converted Mann to Christianity were Maughold, German, Lonan, Ronan, Conchan, Braddan, Adamnan and Bridget, whose names live on in farm-names, holy wells, keeills, parish churches and parishes.

The Vikings

The arrival of the Vikings towards the close of the 8th century brought a great change. The Danes first appeared on the east side of England in 787, whilst about the same time Norwegian pirates crept down the west coast of Scotland. Their first recorded visit to Mann was in 798 when they sacked Inis Patrick.

After the sacking of Inis Patrick, the Island was governed by a succession of Norse kings, among them Ragnall, Ketil, Helgi, Anlaf and Macon. After Macon's death, a period of incessant internal warfare ensued. Seizing the opportunity of this unrest, Godred Crovan (the legendary *King Orry)*, conquered the Island in 1079 and established firm government, justice, order, law and peace. He ruled as King of Mann and the Isles (the southern Hebrides) from 1079 – 1095 and is regarded as the founding father of the Manx nation. During his reign, he established peace and introduced the Norse system of government, Tynwald, which endures to this day.

According to ancient custom, laws are publicly promulgated at an open-air sitting of Tynwald Court held on Tynwald Hill, St John's in the central valley, on 5 July each year.

Godred died in 1095 while visiting Islay. His descendants ruled Mann for nearly 200 years and he himself is immortalised in the Manx National Anthem, *O Land of Our Birth.*

The Norse settlers usurped much of the best farmland (especially in the northern plain), intermarried with the local women and often converted to Christianity, evidence of which can be seen in the Manx Crosses, which are a hybrid of Celtic Christian symbolism and Norse gods and heroes, to be found in many churches and churchyards

There is a fine examples of Viking ship-burial at Balladoole, near Castletown (SC 246 682).

The Isle of Man was under Norse rule and possessed considerable importance as a base for the oversea activity. They left behind many place names including Snaefell (the highest peak), Ramsey, Laxey, Colby, Sulby, Jurby, Foxdale, Sandygate etc.

The British

The era of Norse rule ended with conquest by Scotland, followed by a period in which the Island changed hands between England and Scotland until 1405.

In 1405, King Henry IV of England granted the Island to Sir John Stanley, whose family held it as feudal lords for generation after generation until 1765 when the British Parliament re-purchased the Island (under the Act of Revestment) in a bid to control the smuggling trade. Mann became a Crown Dependency, with a Lieutenant Governor appointed to represent the Crown, and lost a great deal of its former independence.

The Modern Day

Since 1866, when the Island won a nominal measure of Home Rule, the little Manx nation has made remarkable progress. The tourist industry was the mainstay of the Manx economy for about 100 years, from the 1870s onwards. The decline came with the advent of package holidays aboad. The Island then re-invented itself as an offshore financial centre. It currently enjoys a high level of prosperity as a thriving offshore financial centre, with tourism and agriculture as subsidiary industries. The past 40 years have also seen a revival of Manx culture in terms of music, dance and language, including the opening of the first Manx language primary school, the Bun Scoill Gaelgagh opposite Tynwald Hill, St John's.

4
Island Mystery Tour: The North

It is time to take a closer look at the many strange things that have taken place in the Isle of Man over the years. The format that I use will be simple. In the next three chapters I will take you on an imaginary tour, each time commencing from Douglas, the capital and main port, where most visitors stay. These three journeys will be to the north, to the centre and finally to the south. Each area has its own rich legacy of undeniably odd events. Given the relatively short distances involved, any expedition can be comfortably completed by car in one day, although you may prefer to allow longer.

The journey will include general directions and map references to allow you to follow the suggested course (even if you never actually visit the Island), so it is well worth arming yourself with a copy of the OS map for the Isle of Man (Landranger 95) or, indeed, any good road map.

At various points along the way I will, as an aside, discuss some of the phenomena that we will meet. A number of the stories are also a little more involved and may require a lengthier diversion than others. But overall the sense of movement out and back towards Douglas will hopefully be maintained. Of course, you can make these journeys solely through the imagination.

Let us assume that you have arrived on the Island and are now ready for your first exploration. You may wisely have chosen to acquaint yourself with Douglas, especially the Manx Museum, before going any further. For our first real trip we should head north towards Snaefell and the land of the *fynoderee* and UFOs.

All at Sea: Port Jack (SC 395 772)

From the centre of Douglas it is easy to follow the course of the horse tram tracks that go north along the main promenade. After that, keep following the coastal highway out towards Onchan. A massive sign stands out against the cliff wall to your landward side as you approach Port Jack, advising you of the presence of the electric tramway station. That line climbs north from its base here towards Laxey and Ramsey.

At this spot, where tens of thousands of holidaymakers board this delightfully antique transport system for their ride into yesteryear, you may be surprised to learn that you are standing at the border of UFO land. For this area, between Port Jack and Laxey is the centre of the Island's fairly prodigious UFO activity.

From this elevated location you can look eastwards towards the Lancashire coast and northwards towards southern Scotland. Across the dark waters of the Irish Sea, project your mind to 29 November 1957 when one of the most unusual close encounters was reported to have taken place.

It began with a sighting at 2.30 a.m. Several witnesses on the Manx coast spotted a glowing orange fireball in the sky. It appeared out of nowhere and crossed majestically above the water, then exploded in a silent flash, seeming to detonate just like a celebratory firework rocket. Curious UFO investigators delving into the case at first suspected that it was merely a piece of debris from space that had burnt up in the upper levels of the atmosphere. This incandescence would occur as the friction of its speedy passage against the air molecules created a spectacular inferno. Such events are not uncommon – several appear in the skies above Europe every year. They last only a second or two, as did this sighting.

However, there was a sequel to this case that casts doubt on such theories. Four miles (6.5 km) out at sea the trawler *Ella Hewett* was engaged in night fishing when it found itself in the midst of this odd encounter. According to the captain, Fred Sutton, and members of his crew, the glowing mass that approached them from the western sky was shaped like a carrot. It seemed to be quite literally white hot with an orange tinge. As it passed above deck the entire vessel was bathed in an eerie glow, like a million luminous insects coming to life. Then, with a flash, the whole thing burst into starshells and vanished into the silent night.

Even weirder was what happened in the wake of this experience. The paint on the bridge of the trawler seemed to have disappeared, leaving only the metallic undercoat. But what could have caused such a dramatic event? Were the crew seeing things or was this a genuine after-effect? Whatever the case the physical traces proved short-lived. The next day the white paint seemed to be back to normal, leaving one to wonder whether the disappearance was a strange optical illusion caused by the glow that had encased the ship, or whether a rather baffling, physical effect had taken place, its origin unknown.

The White Disc: Onchan Head (SC 402 773)

Several further sightings have occurred on the same coastal road, the A11, a mile (1.5 km) or so north of Port Jack. As you drive this highway the winding tracks of the tramway hug the cliffs that climb through Onchan on your left. But look out to your right.

It was here on the evening of 25 October 1966 that another strange encounter took place above the sea to the north (heading out towards Laxey Bay). According to the two witnesses, the object that they saw was a brilliant white oval silhouetted against the darkening sky. It seemed to hover above the water, as if looking down on the fishing boats below. It then continued on its way, heading towards the southern tip of Scotland, near the Isle of Whithorn in Dumfries and Galloway some 25 miles (40 km) beyond. Like so many UFOs it baffled those who saw it and left witnesses utterly amazed.

UFOs

At this point it is worth looking in a little more detail at what research has revealed regarding the UFO mystery – a topic we will return to later in the book. There are approximately 1,000 sightings per year in the British Isles that describe UFOs. This does not mean that what was seen was an alien spaceship, as far too often the media (and some researchers) tend to presume. It simply means that something was seen which could not be identified. They come in many shapes and sizes, but glowing lights and white discs, as described above, are two of the most common.

The vast majority of sightings can be explained after investigation. They turn out to be meteors, balloons, aircraft reflecting the sun and dozens of other cases of mistaken identity. Only about 5 per cent of all sightings defy serious attempts at explanation. What is more, these odd cases concentrate in certain locations around the globe, known as 'window areas' because they seem to be positions where UFOs just pop in and out of our reality. Indeed this is what the mythological creatures such as the fairy folk appear to do – a fact we will need to consider later. So UFOs and fairies may not be all that different!

The area covering the north of the Isle of Man and across to Luce Bay in Galloway is certainly one of these active windows. There have been a number of puzzling encounters in this region, especially given that it is mostly sparsely populated or indeed primarily open sea.

On 28 July 1963 witnesses on both the Isle of Whithorn and the Isle of Man observed a strange event when a large glowing mass appeared above the Irish Sea and disgorged three 'baby UFOs' in the form of tiny balls of light. These proceeded to move around the large object like children dancing around a maypole and then seemed to re-enter the belly of the large mass before it disappeared into the distance.

There is a possibility that what was witnessed here was a military exercise, although the RAF denied it at the time. There is a military base at West Freugh, just north of Whithorn, and mid-air re-fuelling does sometimes occur over the Irish Sea when large tanker aircraft feed fuel down umbilical cords to small fighter jets whilst they all fly in tight formation. Might this have been what was seen in 1963?

That some UFO activity is linked to events at West Freugh, where stealth fighters have been located in more recent times, is a possibility. But it was not the cause of a remarkable event that occurred at 4.30 a.m. on 1 September 1978, when something happened that has similarities to the encounter on board the *Ella Hewett*.

Farmer Tommy Gibson was alerted to a disturbance in his dairy herd at Garrochtrie near Drummore on the Mull of Galloway. The beasts were running around in panic in a way that he had never witnessed before. The cattle were well used to seeing and hearing low-flying jets from West Freugh, so something much more unusual was to blame this night. In any case the objects that Gibson could see – two glowing silver ovals that seemed almost phosphorescent in the night sky – were not aircraft. They glided, making a humming noise as they moved low across the Mull towards the Isle of Man.

Just as with the aftermath of the encounter with a glowing mass above the Manx trawler, there were weird consequences to this second low-level episode 21 years later. First, the cows, previously excellent milkers, stopped giving any milk at all. But the herd recovered after several days. Even stranger, the farmer was astonished to discover that next day his dark hair had suddenly turned silver – an effect from which it never recovered. Odder still, a group of 6,000 racing pigeons had been released from Lancashire that night and were en route to western Scotland, a course that would take them through the narrow gap between the northern part of the Isle of Man and Galloway. None of these birds arrived. Experts suggested that the pigeons – which are believed to navigate using small magnetic sensors inside their brains attuned to local electromagnetic forces in the earth's atmosphere – must have got lost and headed far out into the Irish Sea. But what could cause such catastrophic disorientation? Was it the same energy field that swamped the hull of the trawler?

Some Ufologists have certain theories as to what might be going on in such cases. They suspect that some UFOs have a strong electromagnetic energy field clinging to their surface. This causes the glowing lights that witnesses report, generated by charged particles that become excited, not unlike the gas inside a neon light tube when a current passes through. Witnesses who have come very close to one of these strange glows sometimes report that they felt their hair stand on end and skin tingle, suggesting that a powerful electric charge was in action. Indeed the glow reported around the *Ella Hewett* could be akin to St Elmo's fire, a natural electrical emission noticed around ships' masts when they sail through electrical storms.

This energy field would possibly be sufficiently powerful to magnetize the particles in metallic paint, causing them to separate temporarily, pushing each other apart like a school science experiment with iron filings. This could make the paint seem to vanish until the charge dissipated.

Could this energy field also affect the digestive system of cows and disturb their milking patterns and create chemical changes in human hair follicles, leading to the colour distortion – a sort of electrochemical bleaching effect? All of these options are scientifically credible. And such an electromagnetic field would certainly disrupt the senses of even a well-honed racing pigeon.

What this means about the nature of UFOs is still in debate. Are such effects generated by the propulsion system of an alien craft? Or, more likely, is there a natural atmospheric phenomenon – a rare and little understood form of electrical storm – that perhaps manifests more often in certain locations than in others, hence the apparent window to the north of Mann and over Luce Bay? Perhaps this effect is caused by the geographical spread of atmospheric forces rather than by the flight paths of alien star ships.

The sightings north of Douglas hint at this idea. And, of course, the suggestion that the presence of glowing masses of energy that can stop cows from giving milk is even more interesting in connection with the ancient legends about the Isle of Man. Think of the glowing lights associated with Manannan's mantle or local folk tales that suggest that elemental creatures such as fairies can repay your disrespect for them by preventing your cows from giving milk. Both are a part of Celtic lore, and both may take on a new light. Are yesterday's visitations by

Themselves being updated by modern witnesses who offer descriptions of close encounters with UFOs and aliens instead of goblins and fairies?

To catch a Mermaid: Garwick Bay (SC 435 815)

From Onchan the A11 continues to wind generally northwards around the rocky coastline as it progresses towards Laxey. But at SC 419 803 it merges with the main route from Douglas that comes in from the left, and both roads now become the A2, with the electric tramway continuing to keep pace.

Just before this junction it is worth a stop, a couple of miles beyond Onchan, at pretty Groudle Glen (SC 415 785). One of the Island's smaller glens, it descends steeply towards the sea with a fast-flowing stream, but is especially interesting because a group of enthusiasts have reopened the narrow-gauge railway that runs for a mile (1.5 km) along the side to Sea Lion Cove, so plan your itinerary according to their current timetable. At a point after the roads merge into the A2 you might take a further walk from Ballamenaugh (SC 423 807), to see the Manx crosses, with their unique blend of Celtic and Norse imagery at Old Kirk Lonan (SC 428 794).

Just beyond the road toward the crosses at Ballamenaugh, the A2 and railway both bring you to Baldrine, ½ mile (800 m) to the east of which is Garwick Bay. This is one of the haunts of the *ben varrey*, so don't forget your camera!

A folklorist named Dr Farrell, who researched local legends in 1894, reported that a group of Garwick fishermen, aware of stories about mermaids sitting on the rocks in this cove, arranged nets in a line across the bay hoping to take one unawares. After several attempts they were allegedly rewarded when one became entangled the next morning. So began the legend of the *ben varrey* of Garwick Bay.

Mermaids (and to a lesser degree mermen) have been a part of the folklore of almost every seafaring race since records began. They are particularly common in Celtic lore. They are nearly always said to possess the upper body of a human woman (with long hair) and the lower half of a fish, or sometimes a seal. Indeed, in the northern isles there are 'seal folk' or *selkies* – who are believed to be humans turned into seals by magic. The *ben varrey* sit on rocks, sometimes singing to enchant men and lure them to their deaths. The legend may have arisen from cases where early explorers went too close to tidal pools and drowned after seeing a dolphin or seal in the distance. Their demise, caused by lack of self caution, was ascribed to the misperceived creature that they were pursuing immediately before.

There seems little doubt that mermaid sightings are based on some real animal and not pure myth. They are too widespread and persistent. Some may be due to mistaken sightings of rarer creatures in local waters such as dolphins, which are uncommon, but are recorded visitors to Manx waters. Interestingly, many of the reports speak of mermaid hair resembling seaweed, perhaps suggesting that marine animals have caught some of this on their head as they surfaced and then looked very strange when viewed from a distance.

In any case, the intrepid Victorian fishermen of Garwick were in no doubt that the creature they had caught was a mermaid. But how much of their story is based on an actual event and how much on subsequent myth fostered by word of mouth retelling is hard to decide. The mermaid was reputedly taken to a nearby hut and cared for by a widow and her son. He fell madly in love with the creature but could tell from her sad yet silent expression that she was not at home on land. So he covertly took her back to the bay to release her from capture. Witnesses say they heard a terrible screaming as he did so and neither the mermaid nor the youth were ever seen again. This part of Garwick Bay was feared as a result of this foolhardy attempt to catch a mermaid.

Sightings of mermaids continue to come from almost every part of the world, even in the present day. They are especially prevalent in the Western Isles of Scotland. For instance, in 1947 there was a well-documented sighting on the Isle of Muck. An elderly fisherman swore he saw a mermaid for several minutes in the classic pose of brushing her matted hair.

Sightings of the *ben varrey* have become rare in recent years but there was a rash of them in 1961, when even a local female civic dignitary in Peel claimed to have seen one on the rocks. Evidently undaunted by the legend of Garwick Bay the tourist board decided to offer a prize to anyone who could catch one of these creatures using humane means (preferably alive in a net). They even went so far as to put an advert in a British newspaper appealing for adventurous hunters to come and join the search! One supposes that if Inverness can have Nessie, the mermaid was considered a potentially useful Manx asset. Needless to say, no mermaid is yet on show in the Manx Museum. But few think we have heard the last of the *ben varrey* and fame and fortune surely awaits the first person to capture one, or at least to get clear and unimpeachable evidence, perhaps on film.

The Fairy Flying Saucer: Fairy Cottage (SC 437 833)

From Baldrine and Garwick Bay the A2 continues north and quickly enters the outskirts of one of the larger villages, Laxey, which is one place you should not miss. It is scenic, quaint, packed with interest and absolutely riddled with strange adventure stories. At the very least, plan to spend a few hours here.

Before you enter Laxey there comes a wonderfully named location – Fairy Cottage. This hints at the fascination of this surrounding area and could hardly be a more appropriate setting for a modern mystery story. That is certainly what occurred in this spot on the night of 29 May 1984.

One of the most spectacular UFO sightings that the Island had during the 20th century was reported there at around 11 p.m. The object was seen approaching from the sea over Laxey Bay and hovered as if surveying the waters below. It was not a helicopter, as some later suspected, because both the police and coastguard investigated the report and found nothing airborne to account for the riddle.

The witnesses, a married couple, saw the well-defined object from their home at Fairy Cottage, which looks eastwards towards the bay. At first, two huge searchlights, like massive car headlamps in the sky, attracted their attention as the object hovered. Then it started to move.

The thing flew inland and passed directly above their house in eerie silence. This gave them a clear view of the object, which had a flat base and was disc-like in structure. There were many other lights to the side of the main headlamps, and what appeared to be several streams of vapour emerging from the rear. The object made a curved path over the Island, crossing over Snaefell, the central peak, and then moved westwards, back towards the Irish Sea. Surprisingly no other witnesses came forward to what sounds like an extraordinary episode – although this seemingly odd 'isolation' effect on witnesses is more common in close encounters with UFOs than one might think. And how many of us routinely look up at the night sky?

I do wonder if this might have been a spectacular sighting of one of the military re-fuelling exercises mentioned before, a number of which occurred in the mid 1980s as practice runs for subsequent long-range bombing missions to the Middle East. What was seen as one object might have been the well-illuminated tanker aircraft (very bright lights are used on it to minimize the risk of collision) with smaller planes lined up around it. The multiple vapour trails could be emerging from this close formation of aircraft that would be positioned extremely high in the sky (hence the lack of aircraft sounds down below). Even the reported hovering can occur when such a formation heads towards the witness in direct line of sight. While it is flying directly towards one it appears to stand still, then to move again as the angle changes.

All re-fuelling occurs at great height and is carried out over the ocean for safety reasons, as it is a relatively tricky manoeuvre given the amount of highly flammable fuel and the close proximity of several aircraft flying in the dark. But as neither the police nor the coastguard identified this source (as they surely should have done if such an exercise flew over Mann), this suggestion is but a possibility.

Gaze out at Laxey Bay and try to figure it out for yourself.

'Themselves' Abroad: Laxey (SC 433 847)

The A2 and the electric tramway converge once more in Laxey, and you are sure to want to sample some of the delights of this lovely place. There are pleasant wooded walks, old shops to browse around, a working blacksmith's, and, of course, the world-famous Laxey Wheel, also known as the Lady Isabella, after Isabella Hope, wife of the Lieutenant Governor, who performed the opening ceremony in 1854.

Laxey Wheel (SC 432 853) is not a tough walk from the tram stop or main road, although it is so well frequented by tourists that there is ample car parking provision closer and alongside if you wish to avoid walking a little uphill. Built in 1854 it is a reminder of a bygone age, when such wheels were commonly used to pump water from mine workings. At 72 feet (22 m), emblazoned with the triskele (Three Legs of Mann) and superbly refurbished, this is claimed to be the world's largest complete working waterwheel. It commands the wooded hillside with the pretty river and glen running at its foot and climbing into the inland mountains behind. A guided tour is well worthwhile.

The wheel sits amidst the countryside once dominated by Themselves, and this whole area is awash with stories of what these fairies did when they were abroad in the fields around Laxey. Here are just a few examples:

A classic tale told to Sophia Morrison, who collected local stories of this sort over a hundred years ago, was the account of a then very old man called James Moore, who had a strange experience half a century earlier. The family lived in a thatched cottage later demolished to clear the land for the building of the Big Wheel. One stormy night, as the rain pelted down, the family all retired early so as to invite the 'Lil' Ones' into the house for shelter.

This was still common practice in rural areas, where these beings were regarded more as neighbours to be treated courteously rather than as alien things to fear.

In the middle of the night, James was woken by his brother, who told him be quiet and led him to a spot where they could peer towards the kitchen. There they could both see an eerie glow that seemed to be filling the room and hear a humming/whirring noise that emerged from the air.

Next morning, they told their father what they had observed and he said it was most likely that Themselves had come in from the storm and availed themselves of the facilities by using the spinning wheel, which the mother had inadvertently left out.

It is worth noting that if a similar tale were to be told today it would likely be given an entirely different interpretation, especially if it occurred somewhere not as famed for fairy activity as Laxey. Indeed I have personally been told many stories not unlike this one and the context they were given was different.

When a modern day witness sees such a bright light filling their house and hears the strange humming noise emerging from all around they almost always think it is a UFO – and as we have seen, they often do have eerie glows and associated sounds. Any evidence of other-worldly activity that is later found would then be blamed, not on the spinning skills of Themselves, but on the machinations of some unseen extraterrestrial. In so many ways today's ETs are again revealed as much like yesterday's fairy folk.

Another local tale, collected by Walter Gill in the 1920s, further illustrates the connection. It came to him from an elderly sheep farmer, who described an incident at a nearby hill cottage some years earlier. The house was occupied by an elderly woman and a servant girl, who had run off leaving a large amount of spinning work still undone. Daunted by the prospect, the old woman knew exactly what to do – she went out into the fields and asked the Li'l People to do the work for her. By the next day they had obliged, leaving fine gossamer thread by the house from which delicate apparel could be created. Some of these clothes were kept for years, but disappeared into nothing, as fairy cloth is wont to do.

You may wonder how this quaint tale can possibly have much to do with modern stories about aliens and UFOs, but remarkably it does. For there are a number of well attested cases, even deep in the space age, of a strange deposit of gossamer-like thread left strung upon the treetops in the wake of an observed UFO flight. This material is known to Ufologists by the quaint term 'angel hair' and some researchers think it is a by-product of the UFO propulsion system – a sort of atmospheric condensation, like ice crystals, that results from the changes caused by the UFO energy emissions.

It is much more likely to be the fine silk threads that can be spun by some species of spider and are left on treetops and hedges at certain times of year. Indeed, even some of the tales seem to recognize this natural explanation, arguing that the fairies are in league with the spiders and have persuaded them to spin the thread on request.

What seems to be happening here is that a relatively rare natural phenomenon (the coating of the landscape in fine spiders' webs) is being imaginatively adopted across the ages to fit the beliefs of different cultures and eras. Many years ago in Laxey it would be perfectly reasonable to assume that such web spinning was the work of Themselves. These days the mystery is explained away to the satisfaction of other witnesses as being caused by extraterrestrial activity. In both cases, however, there is probably a scientific answer – a simple wonder of nature. How often are other myths and legends spun around natural events?

Fairies

Fairies mean very different things to modern society than they did to our forebears, as recently as the reign of Queen Victoria. We tend to have an image of someone demure like Tinkerbell just a few inches in diameter floating about on wings and casting spells with the wave of a magic wand. But this is a modern and fictional rendition of their nature, partly produced by fundamentalist thinking in the late 1800s in order to turn the heathen belief in elves and fairies into a colourful, childhood fantasy that was harmless. Fairies became associated with Christmas trees and pantomime around the same period as part of an active campaign to both romanticize and diminish the still strong faith in these ungodly creatures as very real entities with abilities beyond our control.

The name 'fairy' is also modern. There was once a wide range of supernatural beings, but this term now casually sweeps them all together, from goblins to spirits and even monsters. The word 'fairy' also has a somewhat interesting derivation. It comes from 'fay-eerie', meaning a strange state of enchantment. So the word literally describes the altered state of consciousness into which one is put by an encounter with these beings and it was not defined as the name of any specific being or group of beings, as we now use it. As we have seen, many other names are often preferred to describe these entities.

Indeed it is the universal nature of fairy belief that is most extraordinary. It is not merely a feature of the Celtic nations of Europe (where this belief has remained strong longer than in many other places) but is global in extent, with outposts such as the Hawaiian Islands and Indonesia possessing similar tales going back into the dawn of their history. In fact most major cultures have long had some sense that supernatural beings coexist with us on earth and yet only occasionally make their presence known. These beings had powers and abilities that seemed magical to us but were normal to them, and could help or hinder according to their whim. When something beyond one's ken took place it was easy and natural to blame it on such beings. But their existence stemmed not merely from belief and folk legend handed down verbally across the generations, it was rooted in countless recorded eyewitness meetings with Themselves' Indeed sightings of elves were so common in Iceland as late as the 1990s that a modern cottage industry grew up around them.

As for appearance, this varies according to the kind of being involved, but whilst there are tales of very diminutive fairies most were the size of a small child. Three or four feet (90 cm–1.2 m) tall, in the main they were hobbit-like in nature rather than insect-like, as in most modern fictional renditions. Wings, flying and the visual attributes of a Christmas fairy are recent inventions rather than a common part of the collected lore of people who claim to have seen them over the centuries. More often they wore green, to blend in with nature, making it harder for them to be seen, and were human-like in most other respects.

Indeed, whilst it may be argued by some that we no longer see fairies (not strictly true, as there are a few modern sightings, including on Mann), in a much broader sense they have never disappeared and have featured regularly in the tabloids and on TV over the past few decades; we have just been calling them something else. Indeed, the little green men of space-age mythology are remarkably like the little green men of past generations, even if most witnesses are unaware of this parallel. The only difference is that today we suggest that they come to us from another planet, rather than a dimension that coexists with our own. Most witnesses who allege that they have seen humanoid entities the size of small children and who pilot a UFO have in most significant respects been describing encounters with beings extremely like the ones that have been reported throughout human history and that we once thought of as fairies.

As we have already seen (and will often see again), major aspects of fairy lore, from the spinning of webs to glowing lights and humming noises, are just the same in modern Ufology. This extends to many other features, such as the difference in the passage of time when in the presence of Themselves (time seems to stand still whilst in the real world it continues to pass) and even that state of enchantment brought about from which the word 'fairy' itself derives. UFO researchers have independently recognized that close-encounter witnesses often seem to enter a sort of weird daze where they seem enchanted and experience reality in a different way. They use the term 'Oz factor', likening the effect to the magical land of Oz, but they might just as well call it 'the pixie dust effect' for it is basically the same thing. It is indeed 'fay-eerie'. All that we have done is update our perception of these entities to fit a modern world.

Or perhaps it is Themselves who have updated the manner in which they choose to show their nature to us. There are believers on both sides of this argument!

Modern Manx Fairy Tales: Laxey Glen (SC 428 843)

At the beginning of the last century belief in fairies was dying out, especially on the mainland, but even so there was great interest in phenomena that were being investigated by the newly founded Society for Psychical Research in both London and New York. Many leading scientists were intrigued by evidence that strange things could happen in realms bounded by frequency ranges outside human perception. Rather than blame this on otherworldly entities, they suspected there was an afterlife of wise souls existing in another dimension. This theory remains deeply rooted in some beliefs but is not entirely different from fairy-belief when you think about it: both conceive of another level of reality populated by unseen beings beyond normal perception. Scientists subsumed their beliefs in the supernatural by seeking to use physics and electronics to investigate and maybe to demonstrate the objective reality of this other dimension. Quite a few are still trying.

Ballaglass

In the Isle of Man (especially in Laxey, it seems), similarly odd things were going on, but the locals were not looking for deep scientific explanations: they still knew exactly whom to blame.

A 19th century report tells of how a Laxey man incurred the wrath of Themselves. Walking home late at night, somewhat the worse for drink, he met some of the elemental creatures in Laxey Glen. In the way of many a modern hooligan, he proceeded to hurl insults at these beings almost without thinking, telling them that they were doing the bidding of dark forces and the devil. Suitably riled, the fairies caused a hail of stones to fall from the sky, injuring the bemused drunkard. He staggered home, but never fully recovered.

Showers of stones still occur today and are being investigated by paranormal researchers. Examples are mentioned in my book *Supernatural Pennines*, where gravel, fruit and water mysteriously fall from the sky. Even by the 19th century it had already become common to relate these attacks to psychic forces – a sort of emotional temper tantrum that used powers of the mind as a weapon. The German word poltergeist (noisy spirit) was adopted for this phenomenon and today it is at the centre of many a haunted house mystery. Opinion is divided between those who allege that a spirit in the afterlife, trapped on earth and unaware that it is dead, is seeking to attract attention by such violent acts. Others suspect that a human causes the effects to occur either consciously (via trickery) or unconsciously (by way of extrasensory perception). But there are very few today who would blame the attack on the fairies, although in many ways it seems just as good an answer.

That said, even in the modern world there are reports of alien contacts that have poltergeist-like effects. In one case that I investigated, the woman who encountered a small humanoid creature that approached her car as she was parked in a lay-by, alleged that strange physical attacks dogged her home in the next few days. Room lights switched themselves on and off, ornaments were tossed about and strange scraping sounds were heard – all classic poltergeist features. She seemed to link these things directly with the aliens, even though there is no obvious reason to do so other than the time factor. The man at Laxey did the same, but the aliens were, of course, considered to be none other than Themselves.

A tale recorded in December 1896 also demonstrates how strange events around Laxey were interpreted at the time. It concerned a man living in a terraced house, like those you pass on a walk to the Wheel. One dark evening he heard a faint sound like the wind, which rose in magnitude until it resembled the flapping of a sail. As the noise increased, the frightened man found himself buffeted by invisible forces, and he even had to grab hold of the corner of one of the houses to prevent himself being sucked into the unseen vortex of energy – literally dragged off his feet into the air. Needless to say he was certain that dark forces sent by the elemental denizens of Laxey were at work.

When the terror was passed he walked into one of the houses, shaken and with a ghostly pallor, telling his neighbour (speaking in Manx, so as not to alert the man's non-Manx-speaking wife) that he had just witnessed a spectral funeral. So-called fairy funerals of this type are quite common in the lore further south on the Island, although they are normally accompanied by some a sighting that involves seeing Themselves take one of their own down a haunted pathway for burial. This was the reason why what amounts to merely weird sounds and unseen suction effects were interpreted as a ghostly funeral in this case. The terrified man thought it to be an omen of the death of his own daughter, who was ill.

In fact the girl recovered, but there was a curious postscript. The house at which his daughter then worked as a servant, and where she was staying on the night of this apparition, was owned by a local man of some means. A week after the events he died and his funeral procession passed along the road in front of the very terrace where that encounter had taken place. Coincidence or premonition – who knows?

Such an episode today would almost certainly not be interpreted in the same way. Indeed, like most paranormal researchers, I have had near-identical incidents related to me by puzzled modern witnesses. They speak of strange forces – sudden vortices of energy – winds from nowhere tugging them off the ground, a tendency to float as if being subjected to antigravity, and all manner of experiences which sound like science fiction. They certainly do not think that they have witnessed a fairy funeral.

Here is an example, told to me by Dawn, the widow of a British colonel, who was driving across the Isle of Mull with two American friends who were part of the same Christian Aid group with whom she worked. It was 8 October 1981, almost century after the Laxey phantom funeral, and, importantly, it was broad daylight. All three witnesses heard a faint wind noise, then saw a misty cloud approach and were suddenly immersed in the same kind of vortex that sucked at the terrified man in Laxey. These three felt their car being pulled upwards by a force that smashed open the boot and disturbed its content. Then, just as in Laxey, the force disappeared and they screeched to a halt on a road in the Salen Forest. Dawn's wind-up watch worked normally afterwards, but both the Americans had battery-powered watches and the car had an electric clock. All three timepieces had stopped working as if this misty vortex was accompanied by the sort of electrical energy field that had affected the *Ella Hewett* off the Manx coast.

Manx Mist

As with other such strange phenomena there is a link with what is being reported right across the ages, but the account is adapted according to how society interprets the cause.

Another intriguing case was recorded by the *Peel Guardian* newspaper in December 1898, having been related by a resident of the parish of Lonan. It was early winter, around November, and 'middlin' dark' as he poetically described it. Walking home through the Glion Dhrink area, he had a lengthy journey ahead. He was singing to amuse himself, but then a steady drizzle began and he sought shelter until it had passed.

He described how, as the rain fell, he 'heard it rattling away in the trees and never dreamt of anything but thinking I would get a bit better shelter'. He was surely not expecting what happened next.

As he entered what he assumed was a hedgerow he became lost in the undergrowth. Then the same mysterious vortex of energy described in previous cases seems to have struck. As he put it: 'Something came over me like and I had to put my hand up to keep my cap on for it would not stop on of itself.' This was no ordinary wind. It was almost like a levitating suction effect – apparently the same sort of force that caused the Laxey man to cling to a house gable or levitated the car in the Salen Forest. Nor was it the only effect on this poor traveller, for he felt that his 'legs and knees went all queer like and the singing was all knocked out of me.' He could feel a presence nearby, but could not see anything. He just knew that Themselves had arrived and that these weird sensations, plus the overwhelming sense of tiredness that now overcame him, was their doing.

The man collapsed into unconsciousness and awoke an unknown time later, lost and disorientated. His first thought was that he was in bed, but in fact it was several hours later. He was collapsed on the ground in a very unsteady state and only after fully orientating himself did he discover that 'they' must have taken him and left him on Glen Mooar, some distance from the spot where he first took shelter.

This fascinating case will strike an immediate chord with anyone who has ever read or investigated cases of alleged alien abduction. It is almost identical to the many modern stories where there is an alleged 'dislocation' in time and space and the blame is laid on UFOs and aliens.

As with the man on the road to Glion Dhrink, there is rarely any memory of the 'missing time'. Today we think 'alien kidnap'. A hundred years ago it was 'being taken by the fairies'. Either or neither could be the truth. There might be a psychological or medical cause. But they are surely one phenomenon. Cases of similar fairy kidnapping are common, although they are sometimes romanticized to include details of trips to a strange realm, which makes the story more exciting to retell. Much the same thing happens today for similar reasons, I suspect – a need to plug a worrying gap in recall which humans detest. Alien abduction tales are sometimes (often unconsciously) embroidered in order to make them easier to relate. Indeed techniques such as regression hypnosis are widely used to try to tease out a memory of what happened. But it is just as likely that nothing happened and the witness was unconscious. Hypnosis readily generates fantasy masquerading as an actual memory and the true nature of alien kidnap is at best uncertain, but few seem aware of that.

When the sort of alien kidnap tale that I have often heard is told with restraint it is extraordinarily like this fairy episode from 1898. It is best to remain dubious if someone 'remembers' more via subsequent dreams, which I suspect may also be a key source of many folk-tale 'trips to fairyland'. These visions build on real encounters, adding rich images to them to make them more exciting and widely retold. This is still true when we see how the more vivid an alien kidnap is, the more the media will lap it up.

A modern case that shows this pattern well comes from Rudyard Lake, near Leek in Staffordshire, a century after the assault near Glion Dhrink. The witness, a highly respected businessman, was driving home from a late meeting on a country road having drunk only coffee – although a great deal of it. Stopping to relieve himself he fell victim to a strange attack by a glowing light, feeling his body start to tingle. He collapsed into unconsciousness then found himself on the ground, weak and disorientated, with a large chunk of time missing whilst 'dumped' some distance from where he first lost all recall. This man sought no publicity, but of course he thought of UFOs and aliens not magic or fairies.

When you strip all modern alien abduction cases to their bare bones they come down to a story almost exactly like that reported on the road to Glion Dhrink. This suggests that today's lore about extraterrestrial kidnapping is little more than space-age window dressing that makes these bizarre phenomena culturally relevant in today's world. In the late 19th century, as we have noted before, the equivalent of 'ET' was one of Themselves. But the associated phenomenon experienced was identical.

It is also worth noting that the physical sensations of powerlessness and loss of bodily co-ordination reported in these two cases one hundred years apart are again common. Regardless of whether we try to ascribe them to the machinations of some unseen entity, or attempt a scientific understanding by suggesting an electrical energy field affecting the neurones in the brain, they seem an integral part of the event. Indeed so long have they been associated with fairy lore that the modern term 'stroke' even derives from it. We refer to this medical condition, where the brain loses control of bodily functions for a time,

Ramsey

in an entirely scientific manner, unaware of its supernatural origin. But it began as 'the fairy stroke' where such effects were believed to be caused by an unseen elemental. In fact epileptic seizures, during which a person loses consciousness and some bodily control, were once widely misperceived as being the result of a fairy assault.

Indeed a still-used phrase 'away with the fairies' implies a dreaming aura and loss of concentration. This is a legacy of that very old belief. Perhaps this tells us that folklore, rather than something to be dismissed as 'old wives' tales', has a great deal of value to add to our knowledge of modern supernatural events.

To come even more up to date with odd events in and around Laxey I thank one of my colleagues, Roy Sandbach, for this story recounted by one of his relatives. It dates from about 1937 and involves a woman named Mina, who lived in Douglas, and her daughter, who was then living in Laxey.

One night Mina awoke to see the figure of her daughter in the bedroom, staring at her with a sad expression. She faded away, or Mina drifted back to sleep, it is not clear which. Mina knew immediately what this meant. Later that day, when two men arrived from Laxey to convey the tragic news that her daughter had passed away during the night, it was not the shock it might otherwise have been.

'I know,' she told them. 'She stopped here on her way to heaven.'

Again this is the kind of story, known to paranormal researchers as a 'crisis apparition', that is extremely common. Many times during the First World War, families of soldiers claimed to have had identical visits at the time they were dying some hundreds of miles away on the blood- and mud-soaked battlefields. It even happens when the person does not actually die but is in emotional distress.

The wife of round-the-world yachtsman, Chay Blyth, for instance, described how she knew immediately the moment that her husband's catamaran had overturned, trapping him beneath the hull in the cold waters of the South Atlantic. She was thousands of miles away at the time but the message reached her nonetheless as some kind of energy wave that crossed time and space.

The late Michael Bentine, comedian and highly knowledgeable psychic researcher, told me that he had often experienced this himself and called it a 'psychic distress flare' sent up by the soul at the moment of turmoil.

That is one way of interpreting these undoubtedly real phenomena. The idea that people stop off to say goodbye on the way to heaven is another. Second sight of this nature, when it occurred before the 19th century (as, of course, it did) was regarded as the work of the Devil or witchcraft, or fairy folk. But again it seems to be the same event. We just choose how we wish to perceive it.

In modern times, because scientists remains sceptical about things that cannot be easily proved in a laboratory, such matters are often written off as a dream or imagination. But it was not true for Mina in 1937 because Manx folk knew, even then, that the world was strange enough to include such things as part of an extended version of reality.

Monsters of the Slopes: Glen Roy (SC 410 850)

There are two ways to see Glen Roy from Laxey: the easy way and the hard way. The hard way involves a drive or walk up the small roads a couple of miles westward from Laxey, climbing the slopes through Baldhoon towards Ballaquine (SC 408 848). The much easier route is to take the electric tram from Laxey. A branch of this ascends from the village through the mountains towards Snaefell summit and allows you to see the glen below in comfort. It is a highly picturesque journey and if you choose a fine day then the view from the mountain top when you reach it can be superb. Even on a cloudy day there is a certain majesty to the scene as you appear to rise into a mist-ridden, mystical landscape, where it is easy to imagine all sorts of monsters lurking.

Monsters there are, and these glens are home to several of them.

One is the water goblin known as Nyker, who lives in Nikkesen's Pool on Ballacoan stream, between Ballacowin and Ballaquine. A deep pool, alleged to be bottomless, it has a legend attached that seems to be of the bogey-man variety. Perhaps it was told over the years by worried parents, hoping to scare their children away from what was obviously a dangerous place to play.

According to the legend, the presence of Nyker was revealed when a young girl from Ballaquine was sent out to look for calves which had gone astray. She was heard calling for them quite plainly, but then a great mist descended and rolled down the valley and shut it from sight. Yet those in the valley could still hear her voice calling through the mist and another voice answering and beckoning her to come to where the lost calves were waiting. She followed the voice and disappeared into Nikkesen's Pool. She was never heard of again.

Unsurprisingly this tragedy was blamed on the presence of a goblin who resided in the pool and whose calls had lured the young girl to her death. This was an effective way to ensure that children steered clear of these waters in future – although, needless to say, there were those who continue to think that there was more to it than that. Some still hear her plaintive cries even to this day. So, as you pass through the glen, listen out for the call of a young girl heading towards the fateful grip of the unseen water goblin.

Interestingly, there are connections between this story and one of

Peel

the Island's more celebrated monsters, who lives in the same location: the mostly benevolent *dooinney-oie*. For centuries it was believed that he resided on the slopes above Glen Roy, an unseen but often heard giant presence whose task was to warn of coming danger, especially that of a storm blowing in off the Irish Sea. When his horn was heard, wailing like a banshee, the fishermen of Laxey knew to come into port and tie up their boats hard and fast, and local farmers rounded up their flocks to protect them from the fury of the gales.

One man, Joe Stevenson was coming home on a moonlit September night when he heard the cry of the *dooinney-oie* and saw something glinting on the slopes between Baldhoon and Grawe (SC 432 839). Going up to investigate Stevenson found an odd implement that he took to be the horn of the *dooinney-oie* still lying there and, whilst he was too fearful to take it with him, he moved it to a hidden location. This act outraged the monster, who unleashed flashes of fire from the sky amidst the raging storm that followed.

Another who offended the *dooinney-oie* did so by yelling at him to stop his howling as he staggered home towards Baldhoon past the slopes of Glen Roy. The man then heard a terrible sound heading towards him, which he took to be the angered creature coming for revenge. The poor drunkard fled across the moors, seeking refuge in the house of a local minister as the only place he believed was safe from supernatural assault. The storm raged outside and showers of scree crashed onto the roof, doing minor damage. But it was widely believed that this limited form of assault was all the harm that the *dooinney-oie* could do – rant a bit and then give up. The creature's castigator came to no further harm, but he was rather careful never again to criticize his horn playing.

In recent times the sound of the *dooinney-oie* has been heard less often and it is wondered if he has forsaken Laxey and gone elsewhere. But many in Glen Roy still hope he will return because they see his presence as a protection against the worst that nature can throw at them.

No doubt to modern ears there is a logical explanation for such accounts. On a windy day, as the first traces of a gale whip up from the sea and the weather changes direction threatening a storm, the narrow gullies that line the glen can cause some very strange noises. It is not at all difficult to see these as being supernatural in origin and the cries of a protective spirit warning the locals that foul weather is brewing.

It may just be the wind on the slopes making unusual noises, but somehow it seems much more comforting to think of a spectral protector standing on the hill looking out to sea, waiting for the moment to sound his horn. So, if you descend through the glen as darkness falls do stop for a minute and listen intently to the silence. Can you hear a faint stirring in the trees? Is that noise you hear really just the wind or is it the cry of the *dooinney-oie*?

Good Eggs: Dhoon Glen (SC 455 865)

As you say farewell to Laxey heading north again, the A2 and the electric tramway continue to keep company with one another. The road hugs the contoured coastline, at first heading east and then back north for another 2 or 3 miles (3–5 km) until you reach Dhoon, where the glen bears off towards the sea. This is one of the prettiest glens, with waterfalls and brooks to savour and close to public transport, but the area is home to some pretty odd things as well.

The glen reaches the coast between Bulgham Bay and Port Cornaa, both cited in one of the Island's most delightful mermaid stories, collected by Sophia Morrison and published in Manx Fairy

Tales. It concerns the Sayle family, who fished from Cornaa and who reputedly befriended a mermaid who used to sit on the rocks in Bulgham Bay.

The father was fond of apples and took some with him in his boat. The mermaid was enthralled by these 'land eggs' as she named them and the Sayles were blessed with good luck so long as he kept supplying her with this delicacy. But eventually the father became too old to put to sea and passed the trade onto his son, Evan, who was unaware of the story of the mermaid.

When he saw her on the rocks he explained that his father would not be coming to sea any more. She told him of her desire for more 'land eggs' and promised good luck in return for a new supply. This, of course, he provided, until wanderlust got the better of him and he went off to sail the world on larger vessels. But before he left he judiciously planted an apple tree on the bluff overlooking the bay in such a spot that its ripened fruit would fall into the sea and supply the *ben varrey* with apples. In this way it was hoped to preserve the family's good fortune.

The exercise apparently worked for a while, but in the end the mermaid tired of waiting for the apples to fall and, missing her friendly fisherman, allegedly pined away. The tree remained as a legacy of this ancient pact. So if you fancy a spell of good luck you could do worse than offer an apple to the sea at the foot of Dhoon Glen. You just never know.

Maughold

Old Ghosts: Maughold (SC 492 917)

From Dhoon the A2 again runs mostly north through small settlements such as Glen Mona, 2 miles (3 km) away. From here a short diversion east towards Cashtal yn Ard (Mx. Gaelic, 'castle on the hill or height') is well worthwhile. This ancient site, with standing stones, is 4,000 years old. It would be a pity to drive past so close without walking the mile (1.5 km) or so from the highway or tram stop.

Otherwise, return to the A2 and continue north another 1½ miles (2.5 km) beyond Glen Mona to SC 460 911, where the A15 heads off south (first gazing west at North Barrule – see below). Head east in a long loop on the A15, which will bring you after 3 or 4 miles (5–6 km) to the small village of Kirk Maughold, one of the Island's most ancient settlements. The tramway actually turns eastwards away from the A2 just before this junction and the nearest station is at Ballajora (SC 480 906), just over a mile (1.5 km) from Maughold.

There is a lot to see at Maughold, which was named after St Maughold, a notorious Irish brigand who was reputedly converted to Christianity by St Patrick. The churchyard is the best place to see an extensive collection of Manx crosses (of Celtic and Norse origin) and the ruins of several *keeills*. The ancient parish cross is housed inside the church.

In 1874, a folklore collector named Jenkinson described the apparition known as Ben Veg ('little woman'), who is thought to haunt these parts. He reported that she was a spinner who came from Maughold and who earned a living by touring the houses in the area seeking work with her wheel. In return she was given lodgings and paid a small fee, something that with continued thrift saw her accumulate a good sum. Her exact fate is not known but she was supposedly murdered, perhaps because of this money which she kept upon her person. That tragic end seems to be the reason why she haunted the region in Victorian times, especially the slopes of North Barrule where her apparition was seen holding her head as if in pain. She then set off towards a little valley, seeming to try to walk back to Maughold, but on reaching the valley she disappeared into thin air.

Another legend attached to the area was reported in the *Mona's Herald* in 1847. The house of a man called Quayle was attacked by supernatural forces and windows were repeatedly broken. This was no ordinary act of vandalism, however, since after the first attacks a police team, including dogs, went there. Despite an immediate search of the area no human culprits were discovered anywhere near the house.

It was believed that the acts were perpetrated either by ghosts or by Themselves (indeed there was not then much distinction, as many Manx believed that fairies were the elevated souls of the departed and lived in a sort of union). According to local rumour, this was in revenge for the fact that Quayle had chosen to plough a field that had been left fallow for as long as could be remembered and was a region sacred to otherworldly forces. Bones had been exposed during Quayle's unwise dig.

Creatures of the Night: Ramsey (SC 448 944)

Leave Maughold and go west on the A15. You soon rejoin the A2 around the settlement of Ballure (SC 463 932). Shortly afterwards you reach Ramsey, the main town in the north of the Island.

This is a good place to get refreshment, do some shopping or walk around the pretty harbour. It is also the terminus of the electric tramway. The old steam railway once ran from here to Peel, but the track was ripped up in the late 1960s. So, to continue this expedition you must rely upon your own vehicle or use the bus service, which runs regularly to Peel.

At Ramsey you also touch base for the first time with the famous TT course, where high speed motorcycle racing is held for two weeks each May/June.

One of the most famous parts of the TT course is the Hairpin (SC 449 934), a short way out of Ramsey on the climb to the Snaefell Mountain Road. It is near here that a spectral creature has been seen.

The Hairpin is close to the entrance to the delightfully named Elfin Glen. Its name, of course, is symbolic of the various elemental beings that are said to exist in this typical north Manx landscape. Climb to the Albert Tower at the summit for wonderful views over the northern plain and towards the far tip (Point of Ayre) and even out towards the south of Scotland. It is probably a fine location for a UFO skywatch if you are feeling brave one summer's eve.

In 1859 there were reports of a monster in the form of the demon water bull, the *tarroo-ushtey*, in a pool in Ballure Glen, south-east of the Hairpin. Although the story spread like wildfire and residents from Ramsey rushed to see this beast, it had vanished into the night. It was to reappear later, but a little further north, as we shall see shortly.

The other monster that frequented this area was a black dog. Although sightings of such wild, red-eyed monsters are common throughout the British Isles, the Manx version, the *moddey dhoo*, is exceptionally well recorded, notably at Peel Castle (see Chapter 5). However, it made two much later appearances in Ramsey during the 20th century.

Both occurred in the same place – the road to Milntown (SC 445 943), which heads west out of Ramsey on the main route towards Kirk Michael. Milntown, with its historic mansion and extensive gardens,

Bradda Head

now open to the public, is the centre of much strange activity and also marks the entrance to the deeply haunted Glen Auldyn.

The sightings of the *moddey dhoo* on the Milntown road began in 1927 when a friend of the celebrated folklorist Walter Gill told of meeting the creature as he walked home. He described the beast as a large and ferocious-looking dog, jet black with shaggy hair and eyes that glowed like the embers of a coal fire. It stood as if protecting the highway ahead and the man was too afraid to challenge it. However, after a few minutes, the creature moved aside.

Black dog encounters are widely perceived as ill omens and this man was sure that it had been a warning of doom, as his father died shortly afterwards.

The second sighting, four years later, occurred on the same road and involved a doctor on his way to treat a seriously ill patient. He must have been able to pass by, for, according to his testimony, the creature was guarding the roadway when he returned two hours later after treating his patient. The GP reported that the animal was too large for an ordinary dog – it was more the size of a young bull.

You might wonder if these were not sightings of ordinary wild dogs abroad at night, but it is worth bearing in mind that there are many modern sightings of such large animals on the UK mainland, where the witness has often described something that is like a cross between an Alsatian and a puma. These so-called ABCs (alien big cats) arrive and vanish mysteriously, are often jet black and have fiery eyes.

Whilst countless police hunts have been mounted, these creatures have never been caught and bodies never found. The true nature of this creature has not been discovered, despite modern techniques such as satellite tracking devices. In most respects, these later cases are re-runs of the *moddey dhoo* encounters of Manx folklore.

The Fairy City: Glen Auldyn (SC 437 944)

The A3 west from Ramsey is also part of the TT course, but only a mile (1.5 km) out of town you will come to the B16 at Milntown, which heads south for 2 or 3 miles (3–5 km) past steep-sided valleys and plantations along the course of a small river. This is Glen Auldyn and it is here that an ancient fairy city was said to be located. Unsurprisingly, as a consequence it is steeped in supernatural lore.

There is real history here. Skye Hill, which is the western guardian of the entrance to the glen, was the location of a decisive battle in 1079 when the Norse invaders under Godred Crovan fought the Manx. Before that, whilst the Norse had raided and settled parts of the Island widely, their rule was still not fully confirmed.

After the fierce Battle of Skye Hill, the Vikings took complete control for two centuries, and the north, in particular, is rich in Norse history.

Myth alleges that this hill was important long before that real battle; it is reputed to be where the fairies had a city, usually undetectable to human eyes but became visible at certain times of year. Throughout the Middle Ages and into Victorian times occasional claims of strange lights seen above the hill were interpreted as being the phantom lights of this fairy city. We might wonder, however, if they were UFOs or perhaps an optical illusion.

Glen Auldyn is also the place where the *fynoderee* legend first emerges. According to myth, the *fynoderee* was one of the fairy folk, human-sized and handsome, who made the mistake of falling in love with one of the women who lived in the glen. This dalliance was frowned upon by fairy law, but the last straw came when he decided not to participate in the autumn festival which was sacred to all of his kind, and held every Hallowe'en in the south of the Island. Instead, he stayed behind in Glen Auldyn with his love, an act that his people could not forgive. His punishment was to be turned into a human with matted hair and decidedly ugly features and banished to live in the real world for ever. He had an uneasy existence, trying to help humankind but never being entirely accepted as one of them and, of course, no longer with the rights of a member of the fairy folk.

The magical associations of this area persisted well into the Christian era. For instance, in 1876 Jenkinson was told of fairies the size and appearance of young girls, dressed in blue. Later, Walter Gill collected local sightings that were similar, except that the beings were now said to be small, grey men – something very familiar to today's UFO enthusiasts, by whom little grey-skinned beings are by far the most commonly reported aliens. Indeed the name 'greys' is even afforded to them in this modern folklore. A more precise description of one of the Glen Auldyn entities is that he was the colour of a mushroom or fungus and between 1 and 2 feet (30–60 cm) tall.

Another sighting, early in the 20th century, was made at Milntown and was of a being described as a gnome-like man some 2 feet (60 cm) tall with white hair and a long blue coat. He wore a kindly expression as he wandered towards the glen holding a lantern.

Nor have the encounters ceased, even in the days when fairy sightings had faded into the background. For there are still apparitions in the glen – these days interpreted more in ghostly terms than elemental ones. These episodes centre on the lanes leading down from Skye Hill into the glen, especially around an old mill on the B16 called Tantaloo. Here a figure not unlike a gnome was reported throughout the last century, with a long blue/grey cloak and white head. This may be the same one as the blue/grey gnome with a white beard, although it has recently been described by witnesses as the

Laxey Wheel

Laxey Wheel

misty figure of a woman in a grey cloak with a white headscarf. Indeed, some youths alleged that they were chased by her wielding a frying pan – a somewhat more aggressive posture than the gnome with his lamp!

In 1971 two English tourists reported seeing the figure in Glen Auldyn, and its form had changed slightly again. They agreed that it looked like a small woman in grey. But they could not identify the white object on her head which they say she took off and waved at them! Needless to say they left the area rather quickly without seeking to discover more.

The British ghost hunter Andrew Green wondered if this was an apparition of a woman from the days when the Norse dominated this area, arguing that the white headpiece was not unlike protective clothing worn during that era. But it may be that whatever is being seen in Glen Auldyn is, like so many of the stories throughout this book, identical across the years but interpreted each time according to the images popular in the era in question. It surely cannot be long before the gnome or little woman is reported as an alien. Indeed it is quite surprising that it does not seem to have happened yet – perhaps a consequence of the fact that Mann's heritage already provides a suitable framework for such tales.

Taken Away: Andreas (SC 410 995)

The far north of the Isle of Man is very different from the mountainous interior and much of the south. As we have seen, apart from a small area around Bride it is very flat. It also has some of the best remains of Viking origin.

To reach it from Glen Auldyn, return to the A3 and backtrack for

1 mile (1.5 km) or so to the main crossroads in Ramsey. Then head north on the A9, which takes you some 4 miles (6 km) to Kirk Andreas village.

There you can see the silhouette of the Viking ship burial at Knock y Doonee (NX 407 020), just north of the village, and the burial mound at Knock y Dowan (SC 391 998) just to the west near Ballachrink, (both of which are on private land).

There are also some wonderful Manx (Celt/Norse) crosses in the church at Andreas parish church (SC 415 993), complete with representations of Norse myths about Odin and other gods and heroes.

Professor John Rhys, a scholar of Celtic lore, reported an interesting case from Andreas that dates from 1901. Once again it is a story that will be eerily familiar to those who have ever read any modern UFO tales, yet it was recorded and published half a century before such things were first discussed. The story concerns a farmer's boy named John who vanished one day, to the great distress of his family. Despite a massive search, no trace of him was found. On several occasions they thought that they felt his presence, but he did not return. Odd sounds, such as footsteps and a cracking noise, were then heard around the house without any explanation. The reason for his loss was a mystery for four years, and then the boy suddenly and remarkably returned to the farm. He explained that he had been abducted by the little folk, who took him to fairy land. From there, he could watch all that was going on in his family but could not make contact with them. He had looked on as a mere observer, and was able to tell his stunned parents what they had been up to in his absence, but despite attempts to communicate (the footsteps being one), he could not seem to make himself known. The cracking noise had been caused when he intercepted a fairy arrow fired at him during an escape attempt.

How John returned from fairy land could not be explained. He had lost all sense of time and seemed to lose consciousness as well, simply waking up to find himself back in the real world. He immediately made his way home, where he discovered how much time had passed.

Abductions of children by fairies are common in Celtic lore. Indeed the fairies were said to be especially keen to take young babies or women of child-bearing age to facilitate the rearing of their own offspring. Extraordinarily, this is also a feature of modern alien abduction claims the world over – where the little grey men seem obsessed with the need for human women because of their own difficulties in procreation. That the supposedly extraterrestrial activities of a race of aliens should so closely match those well-recorded activities of the supposedly mythical fairy race is surely beyond coincidence.

Indeed, in a remarkable case from the Shetland Isles, the parallels are so close that there is little doubt as to how this story would have been reported had it occurred two centuries after it did. Here the grey-skinned goblins, much like those reported in Mann, were known locally as 'the grey neighbours' because of their appearance (2–3 feet (60–90 cm) tall and grey).

These creatures showed a special interest in abducting young women, something one poor crofter experienced just after his wife had given birth to their first child. Hearing a terrible commotion coming from the barn he rushed in to discover a group of grey figures in the process of molesting or perhaps kidnapping his wife. He rushed at them with a knife and they fled the scene. She was never bothered again.

Others were not so lucky. In one similar Manx case from the north, the farmer's wife had two children, both of whom were subject of fairy abduction attempts within days of their birth. In the first, the family were disturbed by cries of 'fire' in the night and rushed outside to

Jurby Church

investigate. They discovered that there was no fire and that nobody had called. On their return inside, they discovered the child on the floor, having been moved some distance during a failed kidnap attempt. With the second child, however, the abduction succeeded. This time there was a commotion amongst the cattle in the barn – incidentally a common feature of modern UFO sightings. The father went to investigate but found nothing amiss. Meantime his wife, still confined to bed, struggled to wake the nurse, who was snoring soundly having drunk too much! The mother could thus only watch in horror from her bed as her child floated into the air and vanished, its captors unseen.

She had difficulty persuading her husband that the fairies had taken the child because a baby still remained on the bed of straw where their child had previously lain. But it was not their child, she insisted. This was a sickly-looking, almost wizened substitute left by Themselves – a child that failed to grow normally, would neither eat or nor drink and died shortly afterwards.

Fairy children left as substitutes after a kidnap were known as 'changelings'. Even into the early years of the 20th century the belief in them was strong in both Ireland and the Isle of Man. There were cases recorded of new-born children being seriously abused (and in one Irish case killed) because the villagers were sure that it was not the real baby, but a changeling, and believed that, if tortured, it would be reclaimed by the fairies. Many of these were no doubt children born with tragic congenital illnesses that medical science did not yet understand.

The greys of Ufology again follow the same tradition. There are numerous cases from the 1980s onward (including one that I investigated from Warrington in Cheshire) of women believing that little grey men visited their bedrooms at night. These aliens were then blamed for the strange child that the women later bore (or in some cases just had nightmares about bearing). These children were unusual and seemed to be not of this earth. They had an affected look about them and a sense of superior knowledge that caused them to become known as 'wise babies'. The first known case of this type in an alien context was in Birmingham in May 1959, when a woman gave birth to a child after an alleged alien visit and claimed it was a mixture of human and extraterrestrial DNA.

The parallel between some of the older fairy kidnap or changeling stories from the Isle of Man and elsewhere and these modern accounts of alien abduction is certainly quite bizarre, perhaps even chilling, for it suggests that, at the very least, folklore is a living, dynamic process whose origins and purpose remain unclear. Some fear it suggests much more – that, call them fairies or aliens, these abducting entities are really out there and could be after your child!

Land of the Bull: Sulby (SC 393 948)

From Andreas take the A17, generally south, for about 3 or 4 miles (5–6 km) until you reach the crossroads with the main A3 at Sulby. This is a pretty village with another nearby glen and the A3 goes west from here towards the village of Ballaugh – a famed part of the TT course where motorcycles fly into the air as they cross the hump-back bridge. It is a popular spot to watch the races.

You may like to stop off en route from Sulby to Ballaugh at the Curraghs Wildlife Park, directly off the A3 between the two villages. The Curraghs, which incorporates the park, is a large expanse of protected marshland that is habitat for dozens of species of birds and plants and features in some of the stories that will follow. But in the end you must return to Sulby, as it is here where we will ultimately continue our journey back to Douglas.

The Curraghs is also home to the *tarroo-ushtey*, the demon water bull, of which we spoke earlier. Farmers knew they should treat any representative of 'Themselves' with due reverence, but one farmer from the Sulby area went against this fairy lore and sought to drive the animal away. On each occasion it fled across the marshes towards the sea and disappeared, but the farm suffered grain blight as a consequence.

After seeking help from a local specialist in fairy lore, the farmer remained determined and sought to drive the fated beast from his land altogether by catching it and selling it to an unwitting colleague. He used a rowan (mountain ash) stick to overcome the creature's magic and drove it to the local market. But the other farmers were not to be fooled and told him he must ride the animal and stay on its back, to prove it was tame.

Holding the rowan stick, the farmer attempted to do so and succeeded in riding the *tarroo-ushtey* for a short distance. All went well until, beaming with pride, he felt the stick slip from his hand and the beast, now free of the spell, headed off across the Curraghs towards the sea, the horrified farmer clinging on for dear life.

The beast dived straight into the waves and, aware that it was now or never, the exhausted farmer leapt from its back into the water. He narrowly escaped from drowning and the legend of the *tarroo-ushtey* was well and truly established.

Manx time

Crop Circles

This part of the Island is the only one to my knowledge to have generated any reports of the mysterious crop circles which proliferate on the mainland. A simple circle was reported in a field between Jurby and Sulby in the early 1990s.

The crop circle mystery has only been publicly discussed since 1980, when some were found in an oat field in Wiltshire. It is therefore often wrongly thought to be a modern phenomenon. In fact documented reports of circles date back at least to Victorian times where they were recorded in science journals. They were not then associated with the supernatural, but were presumed to be the result of unusual wind damage.

Circles form in various fields, but usually those with a cereal crop. The stalks are found inexplicably flattened into a circular shape, perhaps 10 or 20 feet (3–6 m) in diameter, but without the crop itself being badly damaged. Indeed it can usually still be harvested. Such simple circles are surprisingly common and virtually all pre-1980 circles are roughly oval in shape. Dozens of them are today reported in crop fields on the mainland and more turn up every summer. They also appear in many other countries.

The circles that attract press attention and are associated with major supernatural belief systems (usually as symbolic messages planted by aliens!) are of complex geometrical designs. Such patterns formed the basis of the hit movie Signs (2002), starring Mel Gibson. Often they are very hard to see from ground level and many circles would probably have gone unnoticed in the absence of today's air traffic or concerted efforts by spotters.

Many researchers (myself included) think that most of the circles are hoaxes carried out by artists or those just out to play games with the alien message believers. But the simple circles, at least, often seem to require a different explanation, because they have been reported for centuries and were first recorded in times when there was simply no capital to be gained from such trickery.

There is evidence that crop circles were found by medieval grain farmers. Old woodcuts and associated folk stories incorporate legends about mysteriously flattened crops. Intriguingly, but unsurprisingly, these folk tales blame those activities on the works of the devil or the fairies, whereas modern speculation centres on aliens and UFOs. This is exactly what we have been noting with other phenomena.

The Isle of Man crop circle was of a simple design. Surprisingly no joker thought to create a bull-shaped pattern near to Sulby (and so missed quite a trick!). But as no hoaxer has ever come forward, it may have been genuine. Meteorologist and physicist Dr Terence Meaden of the Tornado and Storm Research Unit (Torro) claims that real crop circles form below the slopes of hills where flat land and cereal fields catch a downdraft, just as is found around Sulby. According to this theory, Sulby ideal spot for wind vortices to be channeled by the terrain and perhaps create strange swirled circles in the fields.

Mowing Devil: The Curraghs (SC 365 950)

Certain locations where crop circles have appeared in modern times have been regarded as sacred, possibly for the very reason that the ancients also found them there. That is an argument that Dr Terence Meaden has used. He suggests that sites such as Stonehenge and Avebury might have been built in the form of a circle because their builders had seen crop circles in local fields and considered them to be symbols sent by the gods – not unlike the way many crop circle researchers regard them today.

The existence of folk tales, before the days when science and scepticism were brought to bear on crop circles, is important. In folk myth, the circles appear to have been interpreted in just the same way as when other unusual natural phenomena have given rise to beliefs about the fairy folk.

One of the strongest pieces of evidence is an old woodcut that is a contemporary record of a phenomenon known as 'the mowing devil', which occurred in August 1678. This involved a swirled circle which was found in a crop field in Hertfordshire. We know what was found, not only because the text describes it, but because there is an illustration of a demonic figure with a scythe laying out the swirled crop in this way. A legended tale was built around this – that the farmer had a diisagreement with the Devil who flattened his crop. But the evidence of today's circles puts the story in a new light, suggesting that it might have been an historical event that was unexplained and so was given a topical twist according to the popular folklore of the day.

Incredibly, the Sulby area of the Isle of Man can bridge the very same gulf. For the modern Jurby circle is mirrored by a story about the Curraghs of unknown date but certainly no later than the 18th century. The tale concerns our old friend, the fallen fairy or *fynoderee*. Whether he was simply brought in to explain odd things that were occurring (much like the Hertfordshire devil or today's aliens) is impossible to tell. But in Manx lore he was something of a mowing devil, too.

Many references to the *fynoderee* describe his time when living as an outcast as spending his days mowing the cereal fields around the Curraghs. In one account he mowed two fields in one night. In another, recorded in the late 18th century by the historian, Train, he cut the crop,

Old Kirk Braddan Churchyard

but left it standing too high for the farmer's liking. This farmer, blaming the *fynoderee*, cursed his name and was afterwards the subject of further attacks, in which crops were violently uprooted. Guess who got the blame for that?

Walter Gill, writing 60 years before crop circles were discovered by modern researchers, was baffled by how many of the large farms in this area seemed to have tales of extracurricular mowing activity, which the farmers blamed on the *fynoderee*. Like Santa at Christmas, however, the main question was 'how could one being be in so many different places at the same time?' Or was the *fynoderee* the generic name for a tribe of mowers, rather than one individual? The legend clearly implied that he was just one single banished fairy, but the prevalence of these swirled mowing activities suggested otherwise.

Intriguingly, Gill related the typical actions of the *fynoderee* in terms that match modern crop circles extremely well. The fairy mower did his mowing at the crack of dawn, just as most crop circles seem to form in the early hours in the same way (when temperature changes may cause whirlwinds to appear, or when hoaxers, of course, have the best cover!).

Gill even described how the *fynoderee* mowed the fields like a mini-tornado scouring the earth:

'The concentrated fury of his threshing resembled a whirlwind', he noted. 'He flung the grass to the morning star' and 'could clear a daymath in an hour'.

Look at any photograph of a localized summer whirlwind swirling a crop and you will not find it hard to imagine the *fynoderee* in action.

The folklorist A.W. Moore, writing in 1891, citing a story a century earlier originally collected by Train, added a fascinating twist. He said that because of the activities of the *fynoderee* one farmer struggled to get workers to mow his fields, until a brave soldier came up with a plan.

In order to keep watch for the sudden arrival of the fairy mower this intrepid workman 'commenced in the centre of the field' and then went 'cutting round as if on the edge of a circle' – thus creating an all too familiar pattern!

There is even an old folk song devoted to these events – undoubtedly the first ever to describe the creation of a crop circle. (The translation is based on several versions.)

The fynoderee went at dawn to the round field
And lifted the dew from the meadow.
The maiden's hair and cow's herb
He trod them both beneath his feet.
He stretched out his width across the ground
And threw the grass towards the left.

A later verse adds:

He stretched himself across the meadow.
The herbs in bloom were cut.
The bog bane found upon the Curragh
As he moved his scythe it would tremble and shake.

The *fynoderee* may not yet be gone. Perhaps all folk need to do is watch their fields between May and September and be alert for the sudden appearance of a swirled circle. For if one should appear then it may be the *fynoderee's* handiwork, just as, perhaps, it was hundreds of years ago.

Fairy Flights: Tholt-y-Will (SC 377 896)

From Sulby, you leave behind the mystery of the *fynoderee* and his mowing capabilities. The A14 takes you south and is one of the most picturesque roads on the Island, through the winding Sulby Glen before climbing steeply towards Snaefell. Visibility can plummet rapidly and you may need headlights in the middle of the day, so it is wise to pay attention to the weather forecast when taking this route, especially as the view on a sunny day as you wind up through the wooded glen is superb.

Tholt-y-Will there is another haunt of the *fynoderee*. This story relates to a large white rock at the base of the slope, which is said to have been mysteriously placed there by this hardworking creature to aid a farmer who wanted to build a homestead. The sounds that you hear in the mountain pass are not the wind moaning as it rushes through this valley but instead the sighs uttered by the *fynoderee* during his labours.

2001: A Space Oddity

Sulby Glen and Tholt-y-Will lead you towards the summit of Snaefell, which looms to your left as you approach the junction with the A18 at The Bungalow (SC 396 867). The A18 is part of the TT course once again and this is another celebrated viewing spot, especially for photographers. The telecommunications masts on top of Snaefell, are at the heart of one of the Island's most recent mysteries. For this is where a UFO crashed.

In UFO circles the name Roswell is infamous. This New Mexico town was at the centre of a huge controversy, when a UFO is said to

Castletown

have crashed in the nearby desert in July 1947 and the debris was recovered by the US military at the Army Air Force base. Whilst nobody questions that something did crash, the debate is over precisely what it was, continues today.

Eyewitnesses suggest that it was an alien craft, whilst the authorities quickly claimed it was merely a weather balloon. An official enquiry almost 50 years later by the independent US government body, the General Accounting Office (GAO), collated all the key records and sensibly concluded that it was indeed a balloon, but not ordinary one. It was part of a then secret project to look for evidence of Soviet nuclear tests by scouring the upper atmosphere.

None of this has stopped the story from entering modern folklore as a case that will intrigue future generations. It has been made into at least two movies, has been the subject of endless TV specials, and even spawned its own TV drama series, Roswell High, in which the (now part-human) occupants of the crash went to school and suffered teenage angst!

What is less well known is that the area of Isle of Man around the Snaefell summit saw a remarkably similar repeat of this celebrated encounter 54 years later.

At around 4.30 p.m. on the afternoon of Sunday, 14 January 2001 three groups of witnesses independently observed something strange in the sky near one of the masts atop Snaefell just above The Bungalow (at SC 397 882). One witness near Sulby saw a small object like a microlight plane that seemed to be flying low over the peak. Another man, at Jurby, reported what looked like fire falling out of the sky over Snaefell summit. He thought it was a distress flare and that somebody was in trouble.

Two women who were horse riding to the south-east of the mountain were about 3 miles (5 km) from the top, near Laxey, but had a good line of vision as they witnessed what took place. They saw the small plane-like object moving very slowly towards the towers. Then it hit the mast and a shower of sparks of fiery debris fell towards the ground with a trail of smoke spiralling around. Convinced that a plane had suffered a terrible accident, they called the police.

The Isle of Man Constabulary took little persuasion that this was a serious matter. They had strong evidence of their own because just before they received the call there had been a loss of power from the mast, which had disrupted the frequencies used by the emergency services and they had to switch to a back-up source for the rest of the day.

An investigation of the tower in what was now growing darkness revealed some evidence of a collision. There were signs of burning and it was apparent that something had struck the mast, yet there was no trace of any wreckage. Perhaps the damaged aircraft had fallen to earth beyond the mountain, possibly even into the sea around Jurby Head some 5 or 6 miles (8–9 km) away.

These fears were enough to mobilize the emergency services. Police, fire, coastguard and civil defence were all put on alert. An RAF helicopter rescue team was also scrambled from Valley on Anglesey in North Wales. These forces searched the area around Snaefell for six hours without any success, suspending the search only at 11.30 p.m. when they were reasonably sure that no aircraft was unaccounted for.

By the Monday morning it was clear that nothing had come down on the Island and full power had been restored. Daylight revealed that the damage to the mast was slight and that if something had struck it, it may have flown on unhindered. But the witness accounts about the smoke trail and the fiery debris remained a concern. To be certain, the search continued all morning but was finally called off at 12.30 p.m.

At this stage the police were working on a theory that pranksters might have caused the damage by launching a firework rocket at the tower, which would explain the flare and smoke trail that were seen. Inspector Carolyn Kinrade, who headed the investigation, launched a media appeal that Monday for anyone who might have been involved but who had left the scene.

Obviously hoping to appease any would-be jokers who might be scared of prosecution if an innocent jest had gone badly wrong, she promised: 'They are not in trouble. We just need to know what happened and make sure that everyone is OK'.

Nobody came forward, but the Manx police did not give up. One of the horsewomen later told UFO investigator Chris Rolfe that the object she and her friend had seen was the size of a small plane, that it definitely struck the tower and that the smoke that spiraled downwards hung in a pall on the top of Snaefell until after 5 p.m. She had told this to the police and accompanied them up the mountain to direct the rescue teams searching for wreckage. Two days after the incident, when the search had officially been over for 24 hours, the police visited the women again and took them from their place of work back to the slopes. Here they were carefully questioned about distances, angles of view and the apparent size of the 'aircraft'.

From what the police said that day, they had now been advised by defence sources that the most likely explanation was that a model aircraft had struck the tower, and as there was no evidence of any threat to life the investigation should be abandoned. Some police sources were suspicious of this theory – hence the decision to get precise measurements from the women. As the women were told, it seemed very unlikely that at a range of 3 miles (5 km) any model aircraft would have been visible at all, let alone seen in the detail that they observed.

That might have been the end of the matter, with the mystery left to

West Coast

simmer and theories to do battle with one another (including another that the UFO was an exploding meteor). But in fact the police may well have been told the truth of a sort. What struck a glancing blow to the Snaefell mast may have been a model aircraft – an extremely sophisticated, expensive and secret one. These objects are known as remotely piloted vehicles (RPVs), and are intermediate in size between an ordinary model aircraft and a small light plane. They would certainly be visible from 3 miles (5 km) away. These craft are very expensive to build but used increasingly often by the military when it would be dangerous to fly over enemy territory. RPVs with cameras can do a spying job without a pilot.

Such is the sophistication of these devices that in 1998 one was flown in secret over 3,000 miles (4,800 km) by remote control from the USA, across the Atlantic, to land on an island off the west coast of Scotland – not far north of the Isle of Man. Britain is one of the pioneers in developing this covert military technology and it is often used as a precursor to an aerial attack on a dangerous country. In 2002, for example, some were flown over Iraq to seek out defensive missile sites, controlled from an aircraft carrier far beyond the range of enemy fire.

Aviation sources at *Jane's Defence Weekly*, the military technology specialists, believe that test flights of RPVs have occurred off the west coast of Scotland. Indeed the remote island of Benbecula is considered one key site. And on 26 October 1996 an incident occurred on another western island (Lewis) that is remarkably similar to the Snaefell affair.

On that occasion, the Stornoway coastguard was contacted by several witnesses who saw an object in the sky over the sea, heard what appeared to be an explosion and observed a trail of smoke spiraling down into the sea. A major rescue operation was launched but nothing was found and no aircraft was reported as missing. However, by chance there was a pre-arranged NATO naval exercise in this area scheduled for the day after the search was abandoned. Observers claim they saw ships from this joint UK/US exercise which seemed to be continuing the search for debris. It is possible that the use of an RPV in the days before that exercise was a secret part of the plan, since these craft are normally used for initial reconnaissance prior to an actual military operation. Is that what happened in 1996, and did the prototype fail, crashing into the sea?

If so, was another of these super-sensitive radio-controlled model aircraft being flown by the military over the Irish Sea in January 2001? And was it this that struck the communications mast atop Snaefell? Chris Rolfe believes so. He even claims that he was told so by an unnamed source at the Ministry of Defence. A remotely controlled drone was said to be on a test flight from Scotland and was recovered from the Irish Sea, where it was found to have gone down with guidance difficulties. The 'model aircraft' story seems to have been a convenient way to mislead the public without telling them a lie – something, in my experience, the Ministry of Defence is expert at. It is also what may have occurred at Roswell when it was all blamed on a balloon. A balloon it was – but no ordinary one.

Fond Farewell: Creg-ny-Baa (SC 392 818)

From The Bungalow the journey back to Douglas is relatively uneventful. Turn right onto the A18 and follow the road towards the capital. In the next 4 miles (6.5 km) or so you pass several famous places on the racing course, including Windy Corner, the origin of which name is not difficult to guess!

At Creg-ny-Baa the road takes a sharp right turn to cruise the final couple of miles into the northern outskirts of Douglas. There are tales of a shape-changing beast around Creg- ny-Baa that some believe to have been the *fynoderee* in an earlier phase of his ethereal life.

One story links the creature with a field between Creg-ny-baa and Slegaby (SC 390 807), where it haunted the area as a strange bull. The witness farmed the slopes of Slieau Meayll near Creg-ny-baa and knew immediately that the beast blocking his path was enchanted because of its fiery eyes and wild disposition. It had also been seen by his father at nearby Lanjaghan (SC 381 816), but was driven off.

Leaving Creg-ny-Baa follow the A18 south into Douglas, which involves a right turn at SC 390 779. This will bring you home and to the TT Grandstand, Glencrutchery Road.

Cashtal yn Ard

5
Island Mystery Tour: The Centre

This expedition will be a little less frenetic than either those to the north or the south. There is not quite so much distance to cover but it is worth devoting more time in any case to take a good look around Peel. And, if you are feeling particularly energetic, windswept mountain walks will take you deeper into the mysterious hinterland than the otherwise excellent roads can do.

The Angry Buggane: Greeba Mountain (SC 317 816)

Head west from Douglas on the busy A1.The 10 miles (16 km) or so between Douglas and Peel, the largest town in the west, can be done comfortably in half an hour.

The railway that used to serve Peel has long gone but a heritage trail follows the old route along the courses of the Rivers Dhoo, Greeba and Neb right into Peel, so that you can walk between the towns if you are up to the challenge!

The A1 is part of the TT course, branching off at Ballacraine. Along the way you will pass through quite a number of settlements, the Island's mild equivalent of a commuter belt. You will pass Union Mills,

Glen Vine and Crosby *en route* to the more rural surroundings around Greeba Mountain.

And Greeba is where one of the most famed Manx legends is set, the tale of the angry *buggane*.

St Trinian's Church (SC 318 803), dates to about 1350, but an earlier keeill, now totally lost, was once built on the same spot – as is the case over much of the Island.

There is a well known legend associated with the construction of St Trinian's. The story goes that every time the roof was put on to the otherwise completed building it was blown to the ground by mysterious forces. It took little time for the locals, emerging from centuries of Celtic folk belief into the new way of Christian thinking, to blame this misfortune on a *buggane*.

These hairy goblins, who were believed to live in underground caves, hated the coming of the new religion, so they were determined to stamp their authority by preventing the church from being completed. After two fruitless attempts to successfully roof the one at the base of Greeba Mountain, one intrepid and Godfearing man promised to put paid to the *buggane's* anger once and for all.

According to legend, a tailor called Tim from offered to spend a night alone in the church as soon as the third roof was erected. In what amounted to a solo 'ghost watch', he defiantly told the *buggane* that he would complete a pair of trousers in the gloomy candlelit surroundings. If he could do so without being driven out by fear, then obviously God had sanctified and protected the land.

Tim was true to his word but when he had nearly finished his stitching there was a roaring and a shaking of the soil and a head peeked out from the earth. Bit by bit, the creature rose, mocking the tailor with such words, 'Do you see my big head?' followed bellows of laughter.

Undaunted, the brave fellow worked on until he had finished, just as the monster rose fully from the ground ready to pounce.

Tim leapt from the church, cursing the *buggane*, but barely escaped before the roof crashed down behind him with a terrible thud. He fled without looking back, the sounds of fury erupting all around him. He headed for the parish church, where he knew he would be safe. Virtually throwing himself onto holy ground, he was just in time. Moments later, an explosion rocked the earth nearby, caused by the *buggane* tearing off his own head and bowling it over the wall. The church has remained roofless to this day.

Interestingly, this legend is not unique. A very similar tale is told about a church in the Scottish Highlands. It is not clear if it derives from the Manx story, or whether both were simply developed to explain to superstitious locals the troubles they had in erecting a church roof in exposed locations. One can easily imagine that the *buggane* was really just a ferocious storm, contemptuous of the flimsy roof on this building, and that, as Tim ran across the landscape, the crashing of thunder and wind would have sounded very like an angry monster. If a lightning bolt chanced to crash from the sky just as he dived into the sanctity of Marown church, who would not imagine that they were under attack?

Whilst these attempts to explain what might have taken place during the building of the church are not nearly as romantic as the tale of the angry *buggane*, nothing will stop visitors going to this area and pondering this wondrous legend for many years to come.

Seat of Democracy: Tynwald Hill (SC 277 819)

Continue west on the A1 towards Peel for another 2 or 3 miles (3–5 km), allowing the TT course to divert to your right at Ballacraine. Soon

QUOCUNQUE JECERIS STABIT
FAIRY
BRIDGE

afterwards you will approach the village of St John's where you will find Tynwald Hill.

This place is powerful and mystical and must be visited. It is compact and often quiet outside high summer – although definitely not on 5 July, when the Island's parliament, Tynwald, meets in the open air, on the hill, and new laws, are read out. Tynwald Day is a much cherished public holiday.

The hill is a cirular artificial mound (80ft in diameter and 12ft high), which probably existed long before the Norse conquest. It has four such step-like levels that are important to its historical use. Running west to east from the hill, parallel with the adjacent road, is the processional way 100 yards (91 m) long leading directly to St John's Church, a simple nineteenth-century building.

The east–west alignment allows for the sun to rise over the church as you stand on the mound at certain times of the year, and to set over the mound as you look from the church. These possibilities suggest connections with the siting of other ancient monuments such as Stonehenge, where stones were aligned with points of astronomical significance.

A *keeill* initially sat where the more modern church is now, but there are plenty of signs that this was an area of worship even further back into Celtic times, which is, perhaps, why it was chosen as the home of the Manx parliament by the canny Vikings in order to build upon that powerful symbolism.

There are burial chambers nearby, dated to some 2,500 years before the Vikings established Tynwald, making this quite possibly, at 3,500 years, the oldest location in the world where religion, ceremony and governance have been practiced continuously.

If that does not instill a sense of reverence then nothing will. The

Giant's Grave, a Bronze Age burial mound, is less than 100 feet (30 m) north of Tynwald Hill and to the immediate south stands Slieau Whallian, a mountain that, as we shall see, has associations with witchcraft and wizardry.

Some archaeologists suspect that the ceremonial mound of Tynwald Hill sits atop an older burial site and was sculpted for use by the Vikings. But its function for the past 1,000 years has remained constant. Atop the upper tier the Governor presides over the ceremony as the Viking king and his priest once did. On the next tier reside the judges (known as Deemsters) and the Legislative Council. The third tier is where the twenty-four members of the House of Keys (the elected representatives of the Manx parliament) are placed. In Viking times these numbered sixteen (four drawn from each quarter of the island) but this number was expanded after the loss of members from other islands such as Lewis and Skye to the rule of Scotland during the 13th century. Finally, the bottom tier is for local church and parish leaders.

Thus are all the Island's dignitaries positioned on the mound to appear before the electorate, not to mention many tourists, who may stand in the field to observe as the newly passed laws are read in Manx and English. Traditionally, the ceremonial procession along the path to the church involved the laying of rushes on the ground. This was not, as one might expect, a Christian addition but in fact a predisposition to Celtic lore as the act was intended as a tribute to Manannan.

The Dark Guardian: Peel Castle (SC 242 845)

Follow the A1 from Tynwald for another 2 miles (3 km) to the outskirts of the city of Peel, with its Anglican cathedral dedicated to St German.

Exploring is always interesting as Peel has narrow, steep streets that slope down towards the harbour, which is built around the mouth of the Neb. The new marina, packed with yachts and other sea-going craft, is a delightful sight, especially on a sunny day. There is a sandy beach to the north and a causeway lined by fishing boats leading to St Patrick's Isle.

This small rocky outcrop is of huge importance, for it is where St Patrick is reputed to have landed and converted the nation to Christianity by defeating Manannan's supernatural hordes. It was also a vital defence point before and after the Viking invasion and thus became the location for two of the Island's most significant early buildings.

The cathedral has parts that date back to around the period when Tynwald was established; although most of what remains originates from just after the departure of the Vikings in the 13th and 14th centuries, when Mann and the western islands were part of the same kingdom.

Indeed, well into the period of Scottish rule most people on Skye or Lewis looked to Peel Cathedral as the centre of their spiritual world.

The castle comes from the same era, but was built around an earlier Viking outpost on this same promontory. From here it is easy to survey the Irish Sea, and no invaders could successfully approach the western coast of the Island without giving the defenders considerable warning.

Both the castle and the remains of the cathedral still dominate the town, looking down upon its harbour in magnificent splendour. In summer, St Patrick's Isle is home to historical pageants and Shakespeare plays and there could hardly be a more appropriate setting.

St Patrick's Isle is not all that there is to see in Peel. The House of Manannan is a fascinating complex right on the quayside, close to the site of the old railway station, parts of which can still be seen. It contains life-sized replicas of ancient dwellings and a Viking longboat, Odin's Raven, so successfully constructed to original designs that it was actually sailed from Norway to the Isle of Man as part of the 1,000-year

Peel Castle

anniversary of the establishment of Tynwald. Through interactive displays, the centre tells the story of the Celtic and Norse periods in Mann and the close association of Peel and with the sea.

This maritime history includes a close look at the herring fishing industry and the Island's best-known exports – kippers. Close by the House of Manannan is a traditional kipper curing house which now serves as a living museum.

It is on St Patrick's Isle that one of the most renowned supernatural encounters took place. Although the tale was popularized by the great Victorian novelist Sir Walter Scott, it was earlier recorded by George Waldron, an Englishman who lived on the Island for a decade in the 1720s, when he was sent there by the English government. He collected curious tales and dated this strange event in Peel to 1666, when the Great Fire and pestilence threatened the English capital and the Civil War had caused both Castle Rushen and Peel Castle to be garrisoned with soldiers.

Peel Castle was at that time heavily fortified and the soldiers had a strict routine for locking up rooms as the sun set and light faded beneath flickering candles. There was one particularly dark passageway that led towards the Captain of the Guard's room, passing through an old chapel. This soon developed a reputation amongst the superstitious troops for being haunted.

The cause of their fear was a black dog with rough curly hair. It would saunter through the passage, enter the guard room and sit in silence until the night was almost over. Then, before the cock could crow, it headed off into the shadows of the passage. It was regarded as no ordinary stray but a devil dog – the *moddey dhoo*.

The soldiers feared the beast's presence and, at the end of the day when the castle gates were locked, no-one would take the keys on his own to the Captain; they always travelled in pairs and took great care to be respectful to the dog.

All went well until one night a guard, having drunk too much for his own good, spoke with the foolhardy courage. He told the other troops that he would carry the keys alone that night and challenged the *moddey dhoo* to prove itself dog or devil. They tried to prevent him but he was having none of it and snatching the keys, entered the passage. Nobody was of a mind to go with him.

Some minutes later they heard the most unearthly screams and howls, but not a solder dared to move to see what was going on. Moments later, the guard returned from the haunted passageway. His face was ghastly pale and contorted with fear. He spoke not a word, then or afterwards. In three days he was dead and nobody ever knew what had happened to him that fearful night.

The Black Dog was never seen in the Castle again – but he has been seen elsewhere on the Island as noted in Chapter 4.

A Sense of Presence: Patrick (SC 244 822)

Leave Peel and head south on the A27 and in under 2 miles (3 km) you will find yourself at the hamlet of Patrick. You are now entering one of the spookiest parts of the Island – made all the more strange because it is relatively remote and devoid of any substantial habitation, at least human habitation! Various strange presences have been felt here from time to time.

A beggar in the late Victorian era, for example, told how he was able to detect whether 'Themselves' had been abroad where the wild moors sweep down towards the sea because they left behind a tangible odour, a 'sort of sour smell, something like what you was smelling in a deep gill on a summer's day'. He kept clear of these places whenever the smell was detected, just in case.

In the winter of 1902 the local media reported that a curious apparition had been encountered in Patrick. Again it was more a sense of unease than an actual vision. A man was walking on the road that passed westwards from Patrick for ½ mile (800 m) towards Knockaloe Mooar (SC 235 822). It was a brightly moonlit and frosty evening, with the utter silence of the countryside his only companion. But suddenly there was a sense that something was very wrong. He was certain that he was no longer alone.

Looking around him he saw what appeared to be a shadow blocking out the moon and plunging the area into total darkness. It was, he said, 'like a thick cloud of blackness' hovering nearby and he felt, as much as saw, that it was the spirit of someone who he knew had died some years before. This elderly woman seemed to walk with him on the road to Knockaloe and he hastened his steps in order to arrive as quickly as possible for, as he said afterwards, you never know what such an apparition might signify. As he passed a cottage on the outskirts of the settlement, the moon suddenly reappeared and the black cloudy shape disappeared.

Spirit of the Waterfall: Glen Maye (SC 236 796)

As you head south from Patrick on the A27 you enter a supernaturally-charged landscape that dominates the next few miles. But be warned, for around the villages of Gordon and Glen Maye, you have ventured into the domain of *bugganes* and water spirits!

When you drive through the tiny settlement of Ballacallin, on your way to Glen Maye, ponder the curious inn sign at the Ballacallin Hotel,

Monk's Bridge

displaying an unusual creature enjoying a jar of beer. This amusing sign was created not merely as a jovial advertisement, but to represent a story that has long been the talk of this part of the Island. It is an adventure that we will come to a little later.

Our old friend the *fynoderee* was once very active in Gordon. He befriended the Radcliffe family, who were major landowners, often doing their mowing and other chores around the farm. An enjoyable tale is also told about his escapades working at another farm on the moors in the lee of South Barrule (the highest peak outside the north of the island) which lies between Gordon and Glen Rushen.

The *fynoderee* had begun to practice a new way of helping humanity – acting as a shepherd on the cold winter nights. On this particular windy night he sent the farmer to bed and promised to round up all the straying animals safely into the barn. This he did after many hours of effort, and told the startled farmer next day that it had been very easy except for one brown sheep that had been especially troublesome. He had been forced to pursue that infernal creature all around the base of South Barrule.

When the mystified farmer (who had no brown sheep) went to the barn to find out what the *fynoderee* meant, he soon discovered what had happened. The 'brown sheep' was a large hare. This old legend may be one of the world's first supernatural jokes, but is a fondly recalled part of the rich lore of Mann's weirdest inhabitant during his half human existence.

Glen Maye has spectacular sea views, especially to the south. You can also reach Glen Maye via the coastal footpath (*Bayr ny Skeddan*) that runs south from Peel, a walk that will not take much more than an hour and a half and affords some fine views.

Glen Maye has a deep gorge that gives the village its name. On the river that runs through the gorge is a notorious waterfall, *Spooyt Vooar*, which has rich legendary associations.

A *buggane* is believed to live behind the waterfall and the locals are always advised to be courteous in case they should offend him. One story tells of a local woman who was lazy in her ways of managing the house and committed a sin that Themselves found hard to forgive – baking after sunset. As she was doing so, a sound came from the kitchen door and in stormed the *buggane*. He swept the poor woman up in his arms and over his shoulder and carried her out of the house towards the river.

Fearing for her life, the distraught housewife could hear the noise of Spooyt Vooar getting louder, and the stream turning to white spray as it came leaping down the rocks. Only then did she recall that she still held the knife that she had been using for her baking. With one swift stroke she cut herself free of her apron and crashed to the ground, rolling down the grass beside the raging torrent and coming to a rest in safety. Meanwhile, with a roar, the unbalanced *buggane* toppled backward into the water. You can be sure the woman changed her lazy ways after that!

The *buggane* has appeared in the area in other guises. Walter Gill, told of several sightings of a calf that would emerge from the bushes near to the river and terrify passers-by with a clanking noise. He also told a slightly different version of the *buggane* kidnap story where the woman is not the wife of an absent fisherman but a servant outside cutting turnips.

The beach at the foot of the river that flows through Glen Maye is said to have been cursed after a family drama involving the landowners, the Radcliffes, who you may recall had befriended the *fynoderee*. Around the year 1677, the coves around there were used by Henry

Radcliffe for smuggling. He was notorious, not only for these activities but because he had married a Catholic woman from Ireland, something which was frowned upon at that time. His family virtually disowned him and tragedy followed swiftly.

The life of a smuggler and pirate was cruel and one day, after carving his initials and the year on a rock in the cove, Radcliffe sailed off on another dangerous expedition in search of booty. But this time he was not as lucky as before. His boat sank and he never returned.

The Radcliffes cast out his widow and exiled her to a hut of stones, that they built on the edge of the cliffs. Forced to live alone and in poverty, doing labouring work on the nearby farms, she is said to have knelt on the sand and cursed the spot. She prayed that the Radcliffe family might suffer terminal feuds and that no heir would ever inherit the land.

The woman lived to a ripe old age, outliving most of the Radcliffe clan. And the curse seemingly worked, for in 1884 a lawsuit split the family asunder and divided all their property. No Radcliffe heir did inherit the land that she had cursed.

The *ben varrey*, who lives in local waters, is credited with having saved many lives. One time, she swam amongst the fishing fleet wailing loudly, 'Sail to land' in the moments before a fierce storm arose. Those who heeded her cries came into port just in time and unharmed. Those who remained to ride out the storm suffered disaster.

Tynwald Hill

The Adventures of a Friendly Mongoose: Doarlish Cashen (SC 234 784)

Amongst students of the supernatural folklore of the Isle of Man, one case is known above all others. Oddly, it is not a part of the usual tourist trail, like the roofless church of Greeba or Glen Maye waterfall, but that is probably because the spot where this remarkable tale arose is rather remote and decidedly desolate. Indeed, if you make the effort to walk across country to reach it, all you will find there these days are windswept moors echoing with the memories of this extraordinary story. The house in question is long gone, as is its very unusual occupant. Or, perhaps he is not.

This strange tale is neither ancient (it occurred in the 1930s), nor of doubtful provenance. That something happened is beyond question. It was investigated by several highly qualified people, and a few of the locals that I have met recalled it from the days of their youth. Opinions vary widely about what it means and it has gradually become subsumed into Island mythology, causing its true nature to be shrouded in confusion every bit as rich as that associated with the *bugganes* or the *fynoderee*. I have little doubt that centuries from now people will still be arguing about Gef, the friendly mongoose, of Doarlish Cashen, without knowing how seriously to take this unique yarn. So it is worth recounting this case in depth, for here we have an example of folklore in the making that offers hope of illumination rarely possible elsewhere.

Doarlish Cashen was a stone farmhouse situated in a very isolated spot to the south of Glen Maye village, several hundred feet up a stiff southerly hill towards Dalby Mountain. The walk is still possible but reveals only the wildness of the terrain, giving a fair insight into how it must have been in the 1930s when communications were less good than they are now. There is still nothing resembling a road that leads up there, just a heavily rutted and barely detectable path. One quickly grasps how lonely it must have been, especially for the young girl at the centre of this adventure, living far from anyone but her immediate family and without electricity, radio or telephone to ease the pressure of such solitude.

Doarlish Cashen ('Cashen's Gap') was a 19th century farmhouse constructed of slate and concrete with a porch and three small outbuildings with corrugated iron roofs. It faced west across the moors towards Dalby and was frequently battered by strong gales. It was once owned by Pierre Baume, a French merchant who left a trust to fund the arts when he died in 1875. The semi-derelict property eventually passed to James Irving around 1916, when he was in his mid-40s.

Although of Scottish descent, Irving, a non-too successful salesman, came to the Island from Lancashire. He was aware of the popularity of Spiritualism, which was of great interest to the masses on the British mainland especially just before and after the First World War. Many who had lost husbands or sons in the horrors of the trenches turned to mediums, who claimed to have made contact with them 'on the other side' and offered great comfort (although sometimes via séances for which they charged).

Some of the wisest minds of the age took these claims seriously. Everyone from scientific pioneers such as Sir William Crookes and John Logie Baird to great writers including Sir Arthur Conan Doyle devoted some of their time to these matters around the time when Irving bought the farm. Doyle effectively became a professional investigator of such things and was most famously duped by some bogus photographs of fairies that were taken by two young girls in a Yorkshire dell around the period that Irving purchased these 45 acres of windswept Manx land.

Irving's wife, Margaret, was from an old Peel family and the couple had found the decaying property on a visit to her relatives. Hoping for a new start, they struggled with the rundown farm and soon put it in the hands of their son, who employed a German internee from the wartime camps to act as his carpenter. These two young men tried hard to get the buildings into a better state of repair. Meanwhile James returned to Liverpool, where he tried to revive his business career, leaving his wife, daughter Elsie and a baby girl, born in 1918, who was given the Manx name Voirrey.

James failed to prosper on the mainland and rejoined the family at Doarlish Cashen. However, he and his wife were forced to run the property alone when their son, who wanted the bustle and opportunity of a big city, went to live in London.

By the early 1930s, as the odd events began to occur, 12-year-old Voirrey was feeling very alone on the farm because her elder sister, Elsie had, by now, left to live in Liverpool. She had only sheep, dogs and chickens for company. It must have been hard for a growing girl.

Her mother, was a tall and gaunt woman with a magnetic personality, according to those who knew her. She believed in the old Manx ways and was aware of Themselves through her upbringing. James was proud and jovial despite his adversity.

Voirrey, meanwhile, was an average pupil at school without special gifts and described by others as moody and reserved. She loved to read, especially about animals, and would get up very early to help on the farm. During virtually the entire course of this story (up to 1935) she had never left the Island or ventured more than a few miles from her

St John's Church from Tynwald Hill

home. Her only friend was her sheepdog Mona, with whom she set up a skilful practice snaring rabbits to help prop up the family income. Given all this, one can imagine how the apparent arrival in their midst of a most extraordinary animal would change this young girl's life for the better.

Of course, many young children claim to have friends that only they can see. Usually these imaginary playmates are human, but Voirrey appeared to befriend a small weasel-like creature, about the size of a rodent, that came to the farm, and ultimately into the house.

The whole episode might have been brushed aside as the fantasies of a lonely young girl fascinated by animals were it not for the fact that the creature was also seen by her father.

From about September 1931 onwards the strange little creature popped up in the yard or the bedroom every so often. Mrs Irving, however, does not seem to have been party to these early encounters very often.

James described the animal as 'like a weasel – yellow' but with a 'bark like a dog' and a 'mew like a cat'. Apart from making these unexpectedly communicative sounds, the creature (which they came to nickname Gef) also seemed to try to communicate in true Spiritualist fashion by making rapping sounds on the wooden boards of the farmstead whenever it came indoors. These echoed in the dank surroundings.

However, this spooky activity was just the prelude. As if tired of such futile attempts at contact, Gef broke entirely new (not to say fantastic) ground in November 1931 when he started to speak! At first this merely consisted of making odd sounds in the night, which soon kept the family awake. James decided to try to tempt Gef further by imitating local wildlife noises and repeating the name of the creature after each one. Soon all he had to do was speak a name and, what they presumed to be Gef, would answer back from out of the still darkness, recreating the sound made by that animal.

It was Voirrey who took this one step further. She read out simple nursery rhymes into the night and the phantom voice repeated them perfectly. It would seem that Margaret was less enamoured of these games than her husband and daughter, no doubt because she had seen this weird weasel but briefly, and never whilst it was doing the talking. She was even less thrilled when the story came out around Glen Maye (Voirrey seems to have talked at school). Local rumour had it that Doarlish Cashen was being haunted by the spectre of a talking weasel. At first, the rather concerned James considered poisoning the beast to end the fuss; but he was apparently told, 'If you are kind to me I will give you good luck', but if not, he would 'kill all your poultry'. The phantom menace added 'I am not evil . . . I could be if I wanted . . . I could kill you all if I liked'.

Margaret never accepted that there was a supernatural explanation. Indeed she told one early visitor hoping to meet the fantastic animal: 'There are no spooks here', insisting Gef was 'merely' a real weasel. But the possibility that it might be something supernatural soon drew attention. On 12 February 1932 a woman in Peel, aware of the story, wrote to the notorious British ghost hunter Harry Price, now most famous for a controversial investigation of the supposedly haunted Borley Rectory in Essex. Price was intrigued enough to write immediately to James Irving, who set out the basic facts in a reply a few days later, including how in, January, Voirrey had confronted the weasel face to face twice in the kitchen. As for what the creature really was, James described it as a cross between a stoat and a ferret, with a clear yellow-brown cast.

By now, James insisted, the weasel had become part of the family but was very independent and came in and out whenever it pleased. It greeted them by using their Christian names and used a high-pitched voice rather like that of a little girl. Few people saw any significance in that.

The regional media saw this as a bit of a one-day wonder. The Manchester Dispatch sent one of the few reporters who was successful in hearing the animal (but not in seeing it – no outsider ever did). As he put it afterwards: 'I left in a state of considerable perplexity. Had I heard a weasel speak? I do not know, but I do know that I have heard today a voice which I should never have imagined could issue from a human throat; that the people who claim it was the voice of the strange weasel seem sane, honest and responsible folk and not likely to indulge in a difficult, long drawn out and unprofitable practical joke.'

It should be emphasized that the journalist merely heard the voice coming from within the room. James Irving told him it was Gef. The hardened reporter left not only with some head scratching but a tip for the Grand National courtesy of the weasel! Only after getting back to Lancashire and thinking it through did he decide that he had probably been duped by a ventriloquism act by Voirrey, who sat motionless in a chair during the conversation, with her fingers up by her lips. The writer never saw them move but noted, significantly, that as he edged closer to the youngster, Gef's voice ceased. Voirrey had a piece of string in her mouth – which, of course, might have been used to cause a resonating voice.

Price was apparently more willing to be persuaded than most locals, who often saw this as an amusing tale but not much more. He sent an emissary to the family within days of receiving Irving's letter. The man sent on this mission (on 26 February 1932) was a racing driver familiar with the Island.

Under the pseudonym 'Captain McDonald' he spent a day

The Ayres

unsuccessfully trying to meet Gef. But as they set off across the dark moors back to the hotel, a voice was heard coming from the darkness asking: 'Who is that man?' James said it was Gef, but although they lingered in the cold for sometime, nothing else occurred.

Next day the investigator returned, hoping for better luck, but after several hours all he had to report was seeing something whiz past his face and hit the teapot. It proved to be a large sewing needle. James said that this was tossed by the animal. 'It often throws things at us.' But all the disembodied voice said during the second visit was: 'I don't mean to stay long as I don't like you.' Suitably reproved, McDonald went home to file a report with Harry Price.

This sideshow was enough to keep Price interested and James Irving sent regular letters over the next three years recounting the latest antics of their resident weasel. However, they soon discovered that it was not a weasel at all, but an Indian mongoose. This surprising fact was confirmed by Gef himself in March 1932, when he announced that he was born on 7th June 1852 in Delhi, and was therefore approaching his 80th birthday.

Gef had become ever more communicative. Margaret Irving left chocolate and bananas and Gef was said to eat them. At first they had called it Jack but found Gef easier to say, and the mongoose expressed a preference for that name. So it stuck. Soon it was revealing its linguistic fluency by speaking in several languages, including Manx and Russian, and singing in Welsh, Hebrew and Flemish. A few visitors heard the voice, but none ever saw the mongoose at the same time. Indeed few saw it at all.

Something of the personality of the creature (it was a rather moody beast) is grasped by the way it spoke to different residents. It called James 'Jim', Margaret was blasted with poetic abuse (she was variously called 'Maggie the Zulu woman, the witch woman, the Honolulu woman'), and when their elder daughter Elsie returned for a visit Gef insisted that he would leave if she returned to live in the house permanently.

Gef regaled the family with tales of his expeditions to places like Ramsey market. He also left dead rabbits outside the house that he claimed to have caught for the family. He even led them to a lamb that had gone astray, saying it was in apology for being rude to Mrs Irving one day.

In 1933 Gef apparntly began to visit Peel bus depot, hiding under the vehicles and eavesdropping on passengers' conversations, which he later relayed to the family to keep them up to date with gossip. He also learned to read the *Liverpool Daily Post* but got upset when a person called Jeff was reported as dead!

The following year, Gef's party tricks extended to a full rendition of the song '*Ellan Vannin*', and discourses on local folklore, telling the family about the life of goblins and their activities. He also started to play poltergeist-like tricks such as locking James and Margaret in certain rooms.

By 1935 it was obvious to the wise that there was a very close relationship between Gef and Voirrey. He rarely spoke unless she was in another room, and then only as a disembodied voice. It was only supposition that the voice came from the rarely seen animal.

Although many might regard all this as suspicious, McDonald and Price seem to have regarded it as evidence that the girl, now sixteen, was a medium channeling the spirit of this mongoose or some entity pretending to be a mongoose. This symbiosis was especially apparent when Gef began to have mood swings and temper tantrums – of the sort that any teenage child going through puberty might have.

Given such a protracted encounter, one might wonder why no hard evidence was obtained. In fact it was. Fairly early on Margaret Irving tried to photograph Gef, but he was not very co-operative. Eventually, in the summer of 1935, Harry Price decided to visit Doarlish Cashen himself to try to secure real proof. With him he took Richard S. Lambert, editor of the prestigious journal *The Listener*. Being connected with the revered BBC and a governor of the British Film Institute, Lambert was a highly respected public figure and was not going to fooled easily.

Even before these two men trudged up the slopes to Doarlish Cashen they had been sent the first alleged proof – some fur that Gef had agreed to donate to science. In March 1935 this was analysed by Dr Martin Duncan, a zoologist in London. He was certain that it did not come from a creature anything like a mongoose but was most likely from a dog, perhaps even a collie.

In April and May more attempts were made to take photographs, but they all failed as the creature refused to sit still and was only briefly seen running along a wall. When Price and Lambert announced that they were coming to the Island Gef did not seem too pleased. He called Price a doubter and promptly vanished. Although he had often gone missing for days before, he had never disappeared for as long as on this occasion and the Irvings tried to stop the two men making the trip, saying they could not be sure that Gef would be back in time. They guessed he was at the airfield, a favourite haunt, plane spotting!

In July, Price and Lambert arrived and stayed three days, but Gef was not to be seen or heard. They took the chance to talk to the locals, few of whom believed in the talking mongoose. They found nobody who had seen it. However, they did at least leave the Irvings with a modern camera and asked them to try to photograph their guest if he

Milntown

should return. Unsurprisingly, he did resurface, uttering the childish cry, 'Well, I've come back', almost the minute the two men had stepped on board the ferry at Douglas.

A couple of fuzzy photos were taken purporting to show Gef. With a bit of imagination one can see an animal on a fence post, but they also look like a dishcloth or glove puppet. Frankly they could have been anything. Gef also agreed to leave paw prints in Plasticine, photos of which were sent to Price to show to a scientist at the Natural History Museum. This man, Dr Pocock, was pretty damning in his opinion. The major differences visible between the supposed front and hind prints were impossible to find in one single creature, so far as he was concerned. He added: 'I do not believe these photographs represent foot tracks at all. Most certainly none of them was made by a mongoose.'

That was the end of the main story. Interest in it rapidly petered out and Price went off to look into something else, whilst agreeing to write a book with Lambert. By the time the war broke out in 1939 Gef was just a memory and the 19-year-old Voirrey had other things on her mind. So, of course, did everyone else, as the Island was once more flooded with internees, whilst the fear of a German invasion mounted.

Unable to make a living and with James and Margaret now quite elderly, the family sold up the farm and moved away. The farm never paid its way for the new owners either, became derelict and was pulled down some years later. Before then, however, in 1947, the new owner claimed to have seen a strange-looking rodent on his land, probably a mongoose, and had shot it! Whether this was true or simply a story he put out to try to get rid of the unwanted legacy of this weird tale, who can tell. Either way it certainly achieved that end.

However, there was a remarkable sequel to the affair back on the mainland. Price and Lambert's book about their investigation (The

Haunting of Cashen's Gap) a modest affair that was reasonably balanced in the telling. But given Lambert's position in the BBC it created great disquiet amongst the British establishment. A London socialite reported him to the BBC governors demanding that he be fired, because his belief in possessed talking animals suggested that he was, as it was delicately phrased, somewhat 'cracked'. In fact the book made no such claims and Lambert quickly sued for libel.

In November 1936 the case was heard before Mr Justice Swift and the jury found in favour of Lambert, awarding him record damages of £7,500. But the matter raised such concerns that it reached as far as parliament and led to a complete overhaul of the BBC practices and the way its governing body was appointed, which still has repercussions to this day.

So what really happened? The family all died without revealing anything further, if indeed they knew more than is reported above. But there are plenty of opinions. Most locals who were around at the time are unsure. Some feel that Voirrey was too uneducated and unsophisticated to have faked this story, pointing to the various languages spoken by the mongoose. Others think it was a ruse to raise the profile of the farm, perhaps to aid in its eventual sale given the family's struggles. But it was not sold at the height of the mongoose story, when it would surely have made most sense if this were the motive; it happened years later, when the tale was virtually forgotten. Also, among the doubters were the Irvings' other children, neither of whom lived at the farm. Gef seems to have known this and threatened to quit if Elsie returned full time.

Amongst the psychic researchers who studied the case in the 1930s there were some weird ideas. A spiritualist magazine in 1937 claimed that during a séance a medium had received news that Gef came from a race of advanced beings living on earth, of which fairies and *bugganes* were representatives, and had taken an animal form, as such spirits sometimes do. Price discussed several other possibilities, from a spirit possession to a poltergeist attack driven through Voirrey as she went through the traumas of puberty. Pubescent girls are commonly thought to be at the focal point of other such attacks of 'psychic' energy. But trickery remained the option uppermost in the minds of most cautious analysts.

Dr Nandor Fodor, a famed New York psychiatrist and psychic researcher, also visited the Irvings, however, and he was convinced the case was real. He said that he could not imagine the family being insincere and he believed they were 'unlikely to conduct a deliberate deception'. He speculated that Gef was a ghost talking through a possessed animal. Indeed the animal even once said: 'I am a ghost in the form of a weasel and I shall haunt you.' These are curious words, however, as one would assume that the entity would know whether he was a weasel or a mongoose – something he later seemed sure about. But in the end, Fodor concluded that Gef was just a real creature that had somehow learned to talk, and to sing and recite in various languages.

Possibly the most damning evidence came in 1932, during the brief interest shown by the local media. J. Radcliffe visited the farm for the Isle of Man Examiner and got to hear (but, as usual, not to see) the famed beast. He became deeply suspicious of the way Voirrey held herself back whenever Gef was about to let out one of his squeaks. Whilst James Irving translated the high-pitched sounds as the thoughts of the mongoose, Radcliffe could plainly tell that the voice was emanating from the same direction as the young girl. 'Without doubt,' he said, 'the sound was human, and there could be only one candidate'.

Indeed he reported that his team back at the office found the whole thing hilarious. 'We laughed over the whole incident for days,' he noted. 'I say laughed, because it was so badly done that it was extremely funny.'

On the balance of evidence, it does seem most likely that this was a practical joke carried along by its own momentum, probably far beyond what those involved ever expected. Voirrey, lonely, fond of animals, with a moody personality and facing puberty without siblings to talk to, had perhaps driven the whole thing either consciously or unconsciously. She probably did so after there were genuine sightings of an unusual looking animal around the farm, to which the residents quite naturally formed an attachment. From then on it probably became a sort of entertainment in place of radio or television. But once the paranormal investigators and the newspapers got involved it was impossible to stop without looking like charlatans.

To what extent Voirrey's parents were involved or even understood what was happening is likely to be forever unclear. Indeed, after a year or two the whole thing may have taken on a life of its own so that the family became unsure in their own minds how true any of this was. If there really was a strange animal around Doarlish Cashen it might not have seemed absurd that it could sometimes talk.

Much the same happened with the two young girls who photographed fairies at Cottingley Beck, Yorkshire, around the same time. They sincerely believed that they had seen fairies, but nobody would believe them, so they faked a photograph with honourable motives – to convince their dubious parents. They cannot have anticipated that the result would cause a sensation amongst paranormal researchers such as Conan Doyle, leading to endless visits, reports and notoriety that made it virtually impossible for them to admit what they had done. Indeed when the girls were supplied with the equipment to secure better evidence on film for the excited researchers, they felt they had no choice but to go along and try, and must have watched in stunned amazement as the debate unfolded all around them.

Only on their deathbeds as elderly ladies did these Yorkshire girls own up – and even then they disagreed about whether they had faked all of the pictures. They explained that they had kept silent partly to avoid being embarrassed and partly not to disappoint those who had invested so much time, money and reputation in their story; but they still insisted that the hoax was based on a supernatural reality, merely one that they had not been able to prove without creating a few fake photos.

If Voirrey did create the legend that is Gef she may have been similarly forced into ever more elaborate plans to stop the truth from getting out, before letting the animal 'disappear' as soon as possible without raising suspicions. One can imagine how terrifying these circumstances would be to a teenage girl . She would probably have tried to avoid contact with anyone who might become suspicious, yet found herself needing to provide evidence to prevent exposure with, no doubt, to her mind terrible consequences. Voirrey may well even have believed that Gef really was doing the talking.

However, given the mysterious nature of the Isle of Man and the other animal spirits that have been reported locally, can we be completely sure that this was only a child's game that got out of hand? After all, as can be seen from the many other cases in this book, Doarlish Cashen is at the centre of one of the most supernaturally active spots on the Island. There could hardly be a better location for such a strange tale to have been set. But then Voirrey would probably know that.

Something else that Voirrey probably knew, given her interest in animals, was that whilst a mongoose may be a strange-looking creature that would certainly cause a stir if seen around any British farm, it was not an unbelievable visitor. They are certainly not native to the British Isles, but they did live in the area at that time.

It later emerged that many years earlier in 1912 a farmer had imported mongoose to run wild on his land at Dalby, across the moors from Doarlish Cashen. A mongoose loves to kill rabbits and they had become a useful asset to this clever farmer. Perhaps there was still mongoose in the area.

Nobody knows whether they have survived; but, if not, something very weird happened in October 2002, as I was visiting this part of the Island. We were driving along the road that skirts South Barrule heading for Glen Rushen. My mind was on the strange story of Gef as we were nearing the farm and I realized that exactly 70 years before to that day one of Gef's remarkable conversations was supposedly taking place on these hills.

Suddenly, out of the blue, I saw a creature on the road ahead. It was brownish yellow and rather like a weasel. It looked for all the world like the pictures I had seen of a mongoose. If it was not, then it was a close relative. Believe it or not this animal stood in the otherwise empty road right in front of our car – thankfully we were moving quite slowly uphill at the time. I let out a stifled cry, but the animal took off at speed and vanished into the undergrowth.

Of course, it is not really very surprising to encounter an animal crossing your path on a rural road. But it was odd to see one that looked like a mongoose in just this location! It was the only animal I saw at such close quarters during all of my time on the Island.

Quite probably there is nothing mystical about this incident, but it nevertheless brought a smile to my lips. I could place myself in the position of the Irvings all those years ago when first seeing a strange weasel on their land and wondering what on earth it was. And I must admit it crossed my mind that if I was going to end by concluding that the origin of Gef was open to a rational interpretation then, of course, I should add that I might be wrong. If I was wrong then maybe Gef was out there somewhere and seeking the last word.

The Haunted Coast: Niarbyl (SC 212 777)

As you leave behind the mysteries of Doarlish Cashen you will nonetheless be able to keep them in mind for quite some time. The A27 south from Glen Maye skirts around Dalby mountain in a long sweeping arc, keeping the home of Gef on the left-hand side for the next 4 or 5 miles (6.5–8 km). You can train your eyes carefully on the verge looking for any next generation mongoose that might happen by. But at the same time there are plenty of other strange tales to consider, on what is a truly haunted coastline.

The best way to get a feel of this lonely region is to walk the coastal path that passes above Niarbyl Bay and the Gob yn Ushtey waterfall. The steep rocks tumble down to the shoreline and offer a splendid view out towards Ireland on any fine day, with the inland mountains to your east. At Dalby a little road takes you the final mile (1.5 km) or so to the coast at Niarbyl, from where you can get a taste of this scenery.

There are many odd tales from the past concerning Nairbyl. The *arkan sonney*, or ghost pig, was once seen here. This beautiful white animal with pink ears roamed the fields, but was left well alone by the farmers, as they believed it to belong to the fairies.

Out to sea, off the little spit that runs into the ocean at Niarbyl, there have been reports of little twinkling lights bobbing on the surface of the water. Two centuries ago it was widely believed that these were the fishing boats operated by Themselves, out to catch a feast just as the human fishermen coming south from Dalby or Peel might do.

South of here, a 3 mile (5 km) hike over very hilly terrain brings you to Cronk ny Irree Laa (SC 224 747), (Mx. Gaelic, 'the hill of the rising day' because fishermen at sea watched the sun rise in the east over its 1,500 foot (450 m) peak). On the summit are the remains of a prehistoric cairn.

The surrounding moors are part of a Manx National Trust area known as Eary Cushlin, where stood a farm so remote that you might not see a stranger for months. A legend tells of a baby born to the daughter of the house 200 years ago. The child was not welcome when it came, and as soon as it was born it died, without anyone knowing of its birth. The mother carried it at dead of night along the narrow path, past Gob yn Ushtey where the waters leap into the bay, to the place where there is a ruined keeill, known as Lag ny Killey (Mx. Gaelic 'church in the hollow') (SC 217 745), which had been undisturbed for 1400 years and more. There she left it alone.

A short while after, fishermen claimed to hear strange wailing noises coming from the vicinity of the keeill and to see glowing lights on the slopes. They returned to Niarbyl in haste, refusing to go out after dark.

All, that is, except for one brave old man, named Quirk. He faced the darkness and drew closer to shore when the wailing sounds began. Putting down his oars he heard voice wailing over and over again, 'I am a little child without a name!'

Pulling in closer, the fisherman plainly saw a little child on the strand bearing a lighted candle in its hand. He scooped up some water in his hand and tossed it towards the shore, blessing the child, saying: 'If thou are a boy, I christen thee in the name of the Father, Son and Holy Ghost, Juan! If thou are a girl I christen thee Joanney'.

In an instant the crying stopped and was never heard again and the light went out and was seen no more.

Themselves have also been reported in numbers near to this *keeill* – usually when the mist rolls in off the sea – like thousands of small voices chattering at once. Locals saw nothing but knew that it was the fairy fleet. There are also tales about fairy music emanating from caves on this coast. One fisherman claimed to have found tiny footprints in the sand amidst a softly glowing light that seeped from a cave near Niarbyl. The footprints have not been seen again.

Fairy Town: Glen Rushen (SC 235 767)

Return to Dalby on the A27, which continues its circuitous journey around the south of Dalby Mountain, until you come close to the track leading to Eary Cushlin (SC 232 767). Here you pass the entrance to Glen Rushen. Not as spectacular, perhaps, as some other beauty spots on the Island, this is nonetheless a sacred haunt, for it is here that the old Manx believed Themselves retreated and created a fairy city.

This part of the Island 'owned' by the fairies covers a wider area than merely this glen. It stretches 5 or 6 miles (8–9.5 km) to the south towards the popular tourist attraction of Rushen Abbey (strawberries and cream amidst the ruins was a highlight of many a childhood trip to Mann for me and no doubt many others). We will look at some of these places on our trip to the south in the next chapter.

Those who live around or pass Glen Rushen know that it is wise to think kindly of the fairies. Glen Rushen has sparked various sightings, ranging from the human-sized, blond, tall, pointed-eared *glashtin*, who seems intent on abducting young women back to fairyland, to smaller entities seen in the stream that trickles down through the glen from Dalby Mountain.

A hybrid story comes from a vagrant walking though the glen in the 19th century, who reportedly saw a brightly coloured fairy cap floating on the water and heard the sound of the fairy horde, including the slapping of their garments as they washed in the river. But Themselves chose to stay invisible!

One couple touring the area in June 1978 heard a beautiful humming sound emerging from the hillside 'like thousands of bees buzzing in unison'. It came out of nowhere, rose to a crescendo and faded into the still air as if it was a passing squadron of invisible insects.

In fact, this sound, seemingly emerging from the earth, is remarkably common. I have come across modern reports of it in the mountains of North Wales, in Derbyshire and in Yorkshire. Indeed, in the Pennines the reports come from an area of Ilkley Moor where fairy sightings have also been made within the past 100 years or so (see my account of these events in *Supernatural Pennines*).

The modern scientific view is that the noise is electrical energy being produced by the dynamo that is the earth itself and leaking out via the rocks as a sort of powerful shock wave that fills the air.

Of course there are those who still think the humming noise is really the buzz of the fairy town at Glen Rushen. In fact some of the old stories from this area (recall the faint whispers of the fairy fishers heard near the *keeill* in Eary Cushlin) are suggestive of the same forces at work. Did they also refer to the noise that was heard in 1978 around Glen Rushen and then imaginatively reinterpreted? Was it merely described as an anomaly like buzzing insects to more modern ears but romantically interpreted in weirder terms in those days when such events inevitably suggested activity by Themselves?

This is also the only area from which I have received a modern report of what can only be described as a fairy encounter, in no way transmogrified into an alien contact as many of the modern 'little entity' sighting accounts tend to be.

It occurred during the hot summer of 1976 and the witness, John Salter, over from Wirral to watch the TT races had taken a ride around the course and was coming home by a different route. He had stopped near Glen Rushen to have a picnic. It was then that he saw something moving in the trees by his side. He sat perfectly still on his motorcycle mount and watched as a figure about 1 foot (30 cm) tall sauntered across the path and disappeared into the woodland, apparently oblivious of his presence.

'It was like a human being but very, very small,' he told me. 'I know it sounds utterly mad and believe me I thought I was mad. I jumped off the bike and thought I must be seeing things. But I swear it was real. It wore a green jerkin, just like the ones you see in Robin Hood films, and a hat with a feather in it. Go on, laugh,' he challenged.

But, of course, I did not laugh. Had he told this story in 1876 few would have batted an eyelid. It was the way things were back then and only to be expected. A century later it did seem faintly ridiculous to talk of fairies. But then this was the Isle of Man and, in particular, Glen Rushen.

South Barrule

Old Women of the Hills: South Barrule (SC 258 758)

Shortly after leaving the woods that surround Glen Rushen the A27 ends at a crossroads with the A36 (SC 247 758). Take the latter road north. It curves across moorland, with Dalby Mountain to your left and South Barrule looming to the right. At almost 1,600 feet (450 m) this is the highest peak in this part of the Island.

South Barrule has a Celtic hill fort that has been excavated and dated to around 500 BC. It also features remnants of earlier settlements, showing that this location was revered by the oldest inhabitants of Mann and reputed to be the home of Manannan himself.

Indeed, this is also the home of the mountain weather spirit, in the form of a morose old woman known as Caillagh ny Groamagh ('the gloomy old woman'). She has counterparts in Celtic lore all over the British Isles (in parts of England, for instance, she is sometimes known as Black Annis). The belief is that she was set on this high point to watch the elements and warn of the weather to come.

There is an ancient belief that the weather on 1 February will dictate the pattern for the months to come. If the weather is poor then the old woman will stay in her lair and ensure that the summer is better so that she can go out and about then. If, on the other hand, it is a fine day then the coming months may be gloomy and cold.

A small crevice on the top of the hill is said to be the mark of the Caillagh's foot, where she slipped long ago.

The Manx Nostradamus: Foxdale (SC 278 777)

This dismal old weather forecaster is not the only supernatural prognosticator of these hills. Follow the A36 for another 2 or 3 miles

(3–5 km) as it crosses the moors surrounding South Barrule. At SC 278 767, amidst wooded plantations, take the A3 north and you are almost immediately in the old mining village of Foxdale (Norse, fossdal – waterfall valley).

Foxdale is surrounded by hills and small settlements amidst the relics of mining that once predominated. It was sufficient to lead to the laying of the only major freight railway on the Island, a branch from the Peel line that fell into disuse once mining ceased in the 1920s. Foxdale is now a popular rural retreat with good communications into both Peel and Douglas.

It was in the hills around this village that another Caillagh lived and whose story is worth telling. This figure is recorded in several places but there is some confusion about it. Indeed different accounts say that it was a wizard who could change form into things such as giants and animals; others say it was a wizened old witch. The latter seems more likely as these parts have long been associated with witchcraft and the name given to this person is Caillagh ny Ghueshag, literally 'old woman of the spells'.

Among the witches and wizards in the Isle of Man, the greatest was said to be Caillagh-ny-Faashag, ('Wizard of the desolate place') who was able to change into any shape he liked, and who lived in a cave in the hills above what was later to become Foxdale. Apart from being a kind of wandering spell caster aiding the locals by creating potions, the Caillagh's penchant was for prophecy. He is said to have predicted events right up until the end of the world. Unfortunately, rather like his much more famous French counterpart, the doctor and astrologer Nostradamus, he couched his visions in flowery language and metaphor which can be hard to interpret.

One explicit prediction was that the River Neb would run red with blood and the seagulls would drink their fill of it. This appeared to be fulfilled in 1098, during a period of transition in Viking rule, when forces from the north clashed with those from the south on the banks of this river just beyond Foxdale. It is said that so many died in the skirmishes the stream was discoloured by blood.

The mining industry that allowed Foxdale to flourish was prophesised in a verse that told how 'the riches of Mann lie hid behind Barrule' and how 'chimneys' would spring up around every house – as indeed they seemed to do when the ore extraction was at its peak centuries afterward.

What then did this wise man see for the times yet to come? Understanding his words can be tricky but he often spoke of the signs of Doomsday to look out for. One of these may well have happened – roadways cut across all parts of the Island with metal horses rushing down them. A century ago one historian noted that this might be a prediction of the railways which had just sliced their tracks all over Mann and so seemed to have fulfilled that prophecy. But today it seems a more apt description of the highways built for motor cars, which are certainly metal horses rushing at great speed.

Other than that, there is the ominous warning that as the end approaches the leaders of the Island will be forced to escape and that by then Scotland and the Isle of Man will be linked in some way – perhaps by a bridge – a tie that will enable those on one shore to shake hands with those on the other. Let us hope that nobody suggests building the Manx equivalent of the Channel tunnel between the Point of Ayre and Galloway – it might well presage the end of the world!

Witch Mountain: Slieau Whallian (SC 281 799)

The A3 heads north through Foxdale alongside the old railway and after a couple of miles crosses the River Neb and meets with the TT course once again at Ballacraine. We left the course here earlier during this journey into the centre of the Island. From Ballacraine you can turn right on to the A1 and within twenty minutes be back in Douglas ready for the final excursion to the fairyland of the south.

However, on the way to the A1 do take a look at the mountain rearing up to your left at the point where the A40 and the A3 split. You can get a good view from the car park on the A1 opposite Tynwald Hill, where you can stop if you take the slight detour by driving 1 mile (1.5 km) down the A40 into St John's.

This hill is Slieau Whallian, colloquially known as Witch Mountain. Peter Hough, an expert in British witch lore, tells me that it is reputed to be haunted by the screams of dying witches, put to death during the Middle Ages, by placing them in barrels lined with sharp spikes and rolling them down the 1,000 foot (300 m) slopes towards a bog. The result, as you can imagine, was very gruesome.

One of the accounts that provoked this legend tells of a witch who used to bless the fleet as it left Peel to catch herring off Bradda Head and the Sound (between Mann and the Calf). She would go into a trance and foresee the weather, advising the fleet whether or not it was safe to set sail. On one occasion she screamed at them not to go, claiming that she had seen a terrible storm rear up out of nowhere. The men, more fearful for their livelihood than of her, jeered at the pronouncements and set sail, only to be trapped hours later as the skies blackened and became as dark as night, a sudden gale blew up and swelled up the waves with foam.

Few survived the storm and only one vessel remained intact, a Dalby boat called the Seven Boys that belonged to seven young men who were all unmarried. They were warned of the impending storm by the *doinney marrey*, the merman, whom they had befriended in the past, and they made it safely to port.

Stricken by the tragedy, folk took this disaster out on the witch by accusing her of not simply foreseeing this storm but of bringing it about by magic. She was trust into a barrel, screaming her innocence and cursing Slieau Whallian for all eternity.

6
Island Mystery Tour: The South

We can now take our final trip, to investigate the mysteries that lie to the south of Douglas. As before, there are plenty of strange stories to recount and one or two weird first-hand experiences that will await the suitably prepared traveller.

The Sound of Fairies: Old Harbour Bridge, Douglas (SC 375 753)

The road to the south leaves Douglas over the harbour. Take the A6 south and west towards Ballasalla. This is the oldest part of Douglas and the steam railway station stands above the steep slopes near the breakwater, looking much as it did when built during Victorian times. It still echoes to the whistle of the little trains that will follow a similar route to your journey towards Port Erin.

These days the main road safely crosses the tidal harbour., were the fishing boats and pleasure craft now vie for space. The huge passenger ferry that moor beside the Sea Terminal, an impressive semi-circular building. In summer, horse trams clip clop along from one end of the promenade to the other, adding to a sense of history. In the days when Castletown was the captail, crossing Douglas harbour to travel south was somewhat hazardous.

George Waldron, writing of his time on the Island in the 1720s, told a story that he heard from a local man. Forced to cross the river during high tide, when the wooden bridge was rather unsafe, he trusted his horse to brave the waters. But as they crossed in the quiet calm, the air was suddenly filled with eerie music – a rich tone, hanging faint on the night, the like of which he had not encountered before.

The horse stopped midstream as if entranced and time seemed to stand still. Then the music ceased and they reached the other side – forty-five minutes later.

Fairies and UFOs

Being entranced in such a way that you lose all sense of time is a remarkably common feature of entry into fairyland. Indeed we still say (without realizing the origin of a phrase) that when someone is lost in a daze they are 'away with the fairies'. It is a very deep part of our subconscious.

Once across the river and heading towards the south you enter the realm of Themselves, where the risk of being 'taken' was considered very real. In many reports of fairy enchantment music and borders are crucial. There is a widely recorded Celtic belief in the 'fairy mound'. Such small hillocks, often artificial, are found in several places on Mann, with names such as Cronk ny Ferrishyn (hill of the fairies). These mounds occur right across the British Isles, and although they are at least 2,500 years old they still are still held as places of reverence.

One such legend story tells of a young man who heard strange music coming from one of these fairy mounds and walked towards it as if in a trance, promptly disappearing from view. His companions outside could hear the music filling the air but could see no sign of where it came from. Sadly they left the site to report what had happened to their friend, only to be accused of murdering the missing man.

Months passed by but no corpse was ever found. However, determined to prove their innocence and to try to rescue their companion, the men made a brave plan. They persuaded the local village authorities to go back to the fairy mound with them and hunt for their friend in its vicinity. They swore that he must have been captured by the fairies.

As one man edged towards the mound, risking disappearing himself, he was held back by his colleagues, who hoped to snatch him to safety should he also start to be abducted by Themselves. As he partially entered an invisible field of energy that seemed to surround the small hill he could see a beautiful glow inside and some strange little figures, which he described as elves or fairies. His friend was in there, too, staring at these small beings but lost in a daze. Grabbing hold of the brave man, his friends pulled him out and the first victim was tugged clear, too.

After his salvation the man first abducted by the spectral music gradually emerged from enchantment and was unaware that almost a year had elapsed in the real world. To him, inside fairyland, secreted within the mound, time had lost all meaning and barely seemed to have passed at all.

There are various accounts of fairy kidnap – indeed we will see another similar Manx story later in this chapter. But it has left its mark in all sorts of enduring myths – including that of the sea siren, whose singing on the shore so enchants sailors that it lures them to their deaths on jagged rocks.

There is also a classic modern tale of an occurrence on the western Scottish island of Muck, dating from 1912, and recorded in 1937 by Alasdair MacGregor. Two young men were collecting wood on the beach when they observed a strange craft floating near the shore. On board was a small woman dressed in green and two male beings the size of children. They emerged onto the shore and led the youths towards a craft where they were given some strange bread and became very happy, as if drugged, and lost all sense of time.

Their next memory was of being back on the shore, the boat and its occupants having disappeared. Their sister, who was worried because of their lengthy absence, found them. They were standing and staring out at the empty sea, with enraptured looks on their faces, apparently in a spectral trance. Only with difficulty did they break free of this daze to relate their adventure with the boat fairies.

What is most remarkable about these stories is that they continue. Virtually every aspect of these encounters is still recorded all over the planet. This includes strange sounds, trance-like state, profound happiness, small beings, strange food or drink, and a sense of dissociation and confusion over the passage of time. Indeed, as we have seen, the term 'Oz factor' has been coined by modern researchers investigating such tales, usually without attempting any comparison with these old fairy encounters.

Modern paranormal researchers believe it indicates that these people have entered an altered state of consciousness, during which they either experience inner visions or can somehow access another reality where weird things occur, one not available to our normal perception.

There is even a case from Arizona where a group of loggers claimed to have seen a colleague, Travis Walton, being kidnapped into a strange craft after being lured in a sort of daze. He vanished in a flash of light and was missing for days. After he returned, totally disorientated, he claimed to have been in a strange land in the company of child-sized beings. Whilst he was away, just as in the old Celtic tale, the other men who had seen him vanish were suspected of murdering him and were subjected to a major investigation whilst the authorities searched for a body. They were only cleared when Walton returned, in a dazed and confused state, to back up their account. This true story became the movie – *Fire in the Sky*.

Today this weird other-worldly reality is interpreted as an alien contact that occurred on board a flying saucer; but that option is no more supported by hard evidence than was the ancient belief that people were abducted into fairyland. It is even possible to view the Isle of Muck case as in intermediary encounter, sharing many of the old features of fairy abduction but with more modern transport (a boat) instead of a fairy mound. Of course, these days the space-age equivalent of a fairy mound or a sailing vessel is a flying saucer.

The parallels between fairy kidnaps and UFO encounters are so great that there seems little doubt that the latter are a continuation of ancient folk tales in a more modern guise. UFO lore is widely accepted on some level by the masses, but is also sufficiently doubted to distance it from actual belief. On the Isle of Man, if you ask most Manx residents they will acknowledge that the fairies are 'out there', but they will not run their lives on the basis that this is a scientific truth.

Say Hello to the Fairies: Ballaglonney Bridge (SC 305 719)

If you take a bus tour around the Isle of Man there is one folklore site that you are virtually certain to pass – Ballaglonney Bridge, officially known as the Fairy Bridge. Since tourists began to visit the Island in any great numbers during Victorian times it has been one of the key features of an escorted visit that they doff their caps, bow, or at least show some kind of respect to the fairies whenever they pass this spot.

The bridge is, in fact, a fairly small structure and easy to miss, especially when hidden by greenery and busy traffic in the summer. It crosses a stream on the main road from Santon to Ballasalla. After crossing the harbour out of Douglas, the A6 soon merges into the A5, which arrives sharply from the right. You should then continue on this road through Newtown and Santon until at SC 310 723 the road crosses the steam railway just above Santon station.

This is a landmark to watch out for, partly because it announces the proximity of the Fairy Bridge, but also because this is a pretty country railway halt, still in regular use by steam trains and very much like the ones once found all over the British Isles when trains ran to time.

Santon station was also were much of the filming of Thomas the Tank Engine took place. The author, the Reverened Awdry located his railway on the fictional island of Sodor, a name derived from the diocese of Sodor and Man, which itself dates back to the Norse era when Sodor (or Sudreys, southern isles) and Man were part of the same kingdom.

After you cross the road bridge over the station approach, within ½ mile (800 m) you will reach the Fairy Bridge. There is a signpost which tells you that you have arrived, but you are more likely to notice it by the way the traffic often slows. Few people pass by without saying hello to the fairies, or in Manx, *'Morrey mie (or Fastyr mie) Mooinjey Veggey' (Good morning (or good afternoon) Little People).*

There is some doubt as to whether the bridge over the A5 is the real Fairy Bridge at all. It is possible that the legend was adapted to suit the needs of the coach bus and the real fairy bridge is further off the beaten track.

Whatever the case, the fact that one should offer respect to 'Themselves as one crosses the Fairy Bridge has become a highlight of any trip to the Island, and not many people are willing to take chances, no matter how rational they may say that they are! Folklorist Margaret Killip, writing in 1975, noted that local officials had gone to extraordinary lengths to ensure that no-one of importance crossed the bridge without bidding welcome.

During a fairly recent royal visit, she wrote, it was arranged for small 'fairies' hidden behind the low stone wall of the bridge to rise up at the appropriate moment and greet the royal car!

In recent times when I have crossed the bridge (and yes, I always *do* say 'hello!') I have noticed a new tradition. Investigation revealed that this started in the lead up to Christmas 1998, but it has now become an all-year-round activity. Apparently initiated by a child who left a note to Santa, it now attracts numerous messages and notes to 'themselves' being tied to the branches overhanging the bridge. Some people even leave little presents in gift wrap or coloured boxes. On my last visit, the many messages ranged from simple requests for good luck to a poignant request for help find a missing pet dog.

In the 21st century, it is hard to imagine anywhere else in the British Isles so visibly reflective of the desire deep inside of us all to reach out for something strange and mysterious that is beyond the grasp of science with all its knowledge and technology. We all need a bit of magic in our lives and here on Mann everyone is happy to oblige. Ballaglonney Bridge proves that legend and mythology are as alive and healthy as they always have been, and not even royalty is immune to their attraction. The beliefs keep pace with a modern world and remind us that a fairy is for life, not just for Christmas.

Cownapping: Rushen Abbey (SC 278 701)

After taking your leave of the fairies at Ballaglonney Bridge, fear not because they will never be far away during any trip around the south. Soon afterwards (SC 298 711) the A5 bends sharply right over the railway to take you the final mile or so into Ballasalla. From here it goes southward to the airport and Castletown but we head north, west, then north again on roads that skirt this pleasant village – most famous for being the home to Rushen Abbey. Although the Abbey itself is ruins, it is the focus of a well-designed interpretation centre. Just to the north is the 14th century Monks' Bridge (at SC 280 705).

Rushen Abbey was a Cistercian monastery built in 1134. It was dissolved in 1540 and most of the buildings that remain date from the two centuries before that.

A fascinating tale from these parts, at least 200 years old, tells of a local farmer who was mystified by the poor milking of his cows, which always seemed to be exhausted in the morning. In the end he decided to investigate by watching the barn to see if any mischief-makers were up to no good. Soon he grew tired and was about to give up the vigil when he heard a noise from among his herd. He was stunned to see the Little Fellows jump on the cows' backs, crack their whips and make them gallop across country.

The farmer followed, keeping a discrete distance, until they reached a mound that appeared in the darkness ahead. As he looked on, the fairies led the beasts through a hole that appeared in the side of the mound. Light seeped from this entrance and eerie music floated in the air, seeming to entrance the animals. Taking his chance, the farmer slid in behind the gathering. Inside, the place was crowded with Little People, young and old, men and women, all decked out for a ball and dancing to the fiddler's music. In another part of the chamber, the farmer's cattle were being killed and roasted for a great feast.

When they were taking their seats, a man whose face he thought he knew, whispered to him not to taste anything or else, like him, he would never be able to return to his loved ones.

At length, a silver cup of wine was passed around the gathering. Taking heed of the man's warning, the farmer clutched the cup when it was his turn, threw the wine to the ground and fled towards the door. He forced it wide and made his escape, with the fairy troops chasing after him. He survived by reaching the holy ground of Kirk Rushen, where no member of Themselves dared follow.

The cup was put on display in the church and it was there for many years, but no-one knows where it is today.

You may have noticed interesting parallels between this tale and perhaps one of the most famous of all children's stories, which you might never have linked with fairies before. This is because the perpetrator is always described as a strange man rather than a diminutive creature. But as we have noted before we have been misled into thinking of fairies as tiny. Just consider the Pied Piper of Hamelin.

Rather like the *fynoderee,* he used to help the locals in a German town, but when not properly compensated for magically ridding Hamelin of a plague of rats he got his revenge by playing music that entranced the local children to follow him into the countryside. Just as with the Rushen cows, which were abducted by the fairies, these youngsters were clearly suffering from the Oz factor, too, and were taken to a door that opened in the side of a hill, into which they all went – all except one limping child, who was unable to keep up with the throng and saw his companions enter in a state of delighted enchantment before the door sealed them in for good.

Fairy lore, especially in Celtic countries, is full of stories of similar kidnaps. Cows, like children, are often focal points of ethereal attention. But once again it is worth noting that almost identical things are being reported in the very different context of modern alien abductions. And I am very sure that witnesses to these events are not consciously aware of the close comparisons with fairy lore that they offer.

In January 1978 I investigated a case from the intriguingly named Devil's Garden on the banks of the River Weaver, near Helsby Hill, a stunning sandstone mound in Cheshire. This place is one of the most active areas for supernatural activity in England and is known by local researchers as Wonderland. This is because Lewis Carroll (author of the Alice stories) was born at Daresbury village in the heart of this small area.

In this case, a group of poachers swore that they saw a small dome-like object in the field, out of which came several small men with lamps on their heads. Some cows were standing entranced as these beings rounded them up with metal bars.

Another similar case is the remarkable encounter of Alan Godfrey. Just try placing his story some 200 years into the past and stripping it of modern connotations, and I think you will see what I mean.

Briefly (for it is a complex story, told in full in my book *Supernatural Pennines*), Godfrey was a police officer based at

Todmorden in West Yorkshire (a place whose ancient name means 'town of death'). In late November 1980, locals reported some cows missing from a farm and Godfrey went to look for them just before dawn. In his patrol car he saw a whirling mound - like shape hovering low above the road ahead. Suddenly he lost consciousness and all sense of time and recovered awareness down the road, with about 15 minutes of time unaccounted for.

The road surface beneath which this mass had sat was dry, while elsewhere heavy rain had made it very wet. But it was swirled into a crop-circle-shaped pattern. A man driving nearby at Cliviger told police that he saw a strange object over the road, and a police team from Halifax, searching for stolen motorcycles, spotted a glow heading for Todmorden.

During the investigation mounted by our research team in Manchester, Godfrey recalled more details of the missing time (via hypnosis conducted by a celebrated psychiatrist). In these he recalled being taken into a well-lit room where there were several figures the size of young children and also a black dog. Alan could only then recall suddenly finding himself back inside his car.

As for the cows, they were discovered in a muddy field right across a main road with no hoof prints through the mud. It was as if they had been magically removed, rather as fairies had done to the Rushen farmer's stock. Is this all coincidence or powerful mythic forces somehow at work?

The Ghost Road: Ballamodha (SC 277 737)

From Rushen Abbey we now head northwards towards Glen Rushen past South Barrule, which we skirted from its northern side on our last expedition. To get there we need to take the A3, which runs like an arrow just west of Ballasalla. It is also possible to reach it via Silverdale Glen (SC 275 713), north-west of the Monks' Bridge. This is a small area of pretty parkland with play areas for children and a fine spot for a picnic lunch.

The A3 runs from Castletown through Foxdale and right into St John's and has been studied in some detail by the Merseyside researcher John Hall, who has sent me copies of his excellent, copious work.

Hall considers this to be a ghost road and has found a great deal of supernatural lore associated with it (and with the A27, which runs parallel to it to the west), ranging from sightings of large black dogs (*moddey dhoo*) to processions of what may be spectral monks heading on a track towards Rushen Abbey. His work has been published in a lengthy series of reports by the Merseyside Anomalies Research Association (MARA) in their fine quarterly journal The Researcher, and I recommend that you read this painstakingly-gathered and fascinating data.

I do not intend to duplicate John's findings here, but will note a few things that I have discovered for myself in this area. In terms of settlements the region centres on Ballamodha and one phenomenon heard but not usually seen near here is a troop of fairies, rather like those that chased the Rushen farmer. The sound is often heard as a gentle roaring noise that rises to a crescendo and fades as it passes. Many travellers on this road in the dead of night have stood to one side, fearful of what might lie behind its terror.

Hall thinks that some of these stories might mask the old smuggling trade routes that led south toward the sea – the smugglers, of course, using this road in the middle of the night to avoid detection. They may have spread the legend about an unseen fairy troop as a way to deter people from venturing out and watching their illegal activities. But he also feels that some tales have a real basis.

One case I discovered comes from a touring couple in October 1966, who were hiking up this road after dark, not far from the South Barrule plantation just north of Ballamodha. They described what they heard as follows.

It began like the noise of a waterfall. We had not seen one of those on our maps so we stopped to discuss where it might be situated, but by now it had got much louder. I would probably have to say that it was like the wind through trees – except that there was no wind. My girlfriend and I stood perfectly still – to be honest we were too frightened to move more than an inch. The sound was plainly going in a straight line to the south. We could follow it all the way. Then it faded and was gone. We decided to abandon the rest of our trip and get some supper – taking a lift to Peel as soon as one became available. Unfortunately it could not come fast enough for my girlfriend.

I walked through the woods by South Barrule just to get a feel of what this experience must have been; although I was not going to do it at night! It was still an eerie experience. Soon after I left the path I was swallowed up in the gloom and felt utterly alone. The quietness was piercing. Then, after a few minutes, my ears became adjusted to a faint noise that emerged. It did sound like running water.

I was persuaded that what I was hearing was just the wind coming down off the slopes of South Barrule and rippling through the thousands of trees. It ebbed and flowed like the tide and I could imagine how at night, especially if one was aware of the legend of the fairy troops, this would take on a mysterious character. Perhaps I am being overly cautious in determining that this old legend is based on the works of nature rather than of supernature – indeed the plantation here is relatively modern – but I discovered something else that may be relevant. I checked out the meteorological records of the area and discovered that small tornadoes are not unknown in these parts. There have been reports in 1997 and 1998 of funnel clouds, from which tornadoes emerge, and waterspouts (sea-borne tornadoes) near both Castletown and Port St Mary, only a few miles south and west of this spot. They appear to be channeled by wind vortices that can roar off the slopes of South Barrule.

Whilst tornadoes are rarely destructive in the British Isles they are surprisingly frequent according to the Tornado and Storm Research Organisation. Indeed these islands are uncommonly alive with such focused wind activity. These violent squalls tend to travel across country and would pass north to south through this area. Most would only be short lived and not visible in any way (especially at night), simply being felt as an unexpected blast if one is in its path, shutting gates or blowing you about. Or one might merely hear the sound that they made as they swept through the trees off to one side, thus feeling nothing.

Consequently if there are dozens of these small and very short-lived whirlwinds focused in this area every year, it is not a surprising that in the past they might be ascribed to the work of the fairies. John Hall reports a case of a man who was pursued near Port Erin by a noise like stones being moved around and he likens this (quite correctly) to a poltergeist attack. However, a sudden transient tornado passing through the fields would certainly have sufficient power to move small stones. So I do wonder if the many cases of this phantom noise on the ghost road, to which all manner of supernatural explanations have been given, might in fact result from the unusual actions of the wind.

Devil's Den: South Barrule (SC 258 759)

On the slopes of South Barrule, beyond the area that is now a plantation was a spot reputed to be home to the Devil – the Devil's Den, in fact. If you take the A36 sharp left off the A3 (at SC 278 767) it takes you through the woodland and hugs the base of the mountain.

According to Waldron (from his research in the 1720s), this area has been at the centre of further fairy music encounters – strange ethereal sounds ascribed to Themselves enjoying the foibles of humanity – at least of those who dared pass along what was then a barren and remote mountain track. This spot is not much less barren today and few cars seem to traverse it, allowing one to stop, get out, listen to the howling wind and try to hear the eerie sound of idling fairies that may yet be mixed with it.

Waldron also heard stories about what was termed 'the time of enchantment', which seems to have been the age when prophets, witches and magicians lived like hermits on the hills around here. The Devil's Den was believed to be a secret bolt-hole in the mountain, used as a sort of supernatural prison, where undesirables (or those out of favour with the magician) were ensnared – presumably until the spell was broken. One prince was reputedly held there for 600 years!

Another interesting legend about this part of South Barrule is the belief that animals can sense the supernatural presence because it is so strong here. It was claimed that if you took a dog or horse to this spot it would stare dead ahead in shock and its hair would stand on end. Waldron even heard one story in which a 'dragon' was seen to 'descend swiftly' into the Devil's Den. It was described as a huge, dark thing with a tail and fiery-red eyes and uttered a terrible noise.

Evidently, odd things were seen in this location that led to its continuous reputation for the supernatural. Not surprisingly, in modern UFO sightings, dogs and horses react similarly in the presence of UFOs. Indeed there are numerous reports where the hairs of a dog or of a human witness have literally stood on end when in the presence of a fiery object. Some researchers suspect that this is a consequence of a powerful electrostatic field that charges up the atmosphere. Witnesses also describe other effects, such as a tingling sensation on the skin and watering of the eyes, which are known to result from exposure to a strong static charge. The energy is emitted by the presence of a UFO (whatever a UFO might be).

It is worth recalling the whirlwinds in this area because tornadoes generate strong electrostatic fields when the vortex rotates at great speed to produce friction. Indeed, the manufacturers of a brand of modern vacuum cleaner designed to suck up dust with an artificial vortex told me that they had to find ways around this problem. The dust acquired such a strong charge that susceptible users were getting a shock! Both heat and red glows result from rotating tornadoes as the dust is swirled around by the vortex. Crackling sounds of electrical discharge are also common. If such mini-tornadoes were seen on the South Barrule slopes with red glows, lightning and fearsome crackles, causing the hair to stand on end, then might not locals have believed in flying dragons in the days before meteorology was understood?

Surely It Must Be a Trick: Magnetic Hill (SC 244 735)

We continue to round South Barrule to the north on the A36 but after 2 more miles (3 km) arrive at the crossroads near the top of Glen Rushen (SC 246 758). The glen itself is worth a visit, with wild scenery which was previously the exclusive province of Themselves to enjoy.

From here take the southern route, the A27, heading for Colby and Port St Mary. You are about to undergo an eerie experience of your own that will prove, as nothing else ever could, that this is an area where fairies and magicians are truly in command.

About 2 miles (3 km) down this road you will come to a small hill not marked on the OS map but shown on some tourist maps as Magnetic Hill. Do not drive through without stopping, you must savour the experience. Unfortunately, you really need to be in a vehicle rather than on foot (although even a cycle is good enough) to experience its true effect.

The hill covers several hundred yards but the key spot to look for is a large quartz-encrusted boulder in the grass by the verge. You will find it on your right as you head south towards Ronague. It is difficult to miss if you drive slowly enough. Stop your car by this boulder and switch off the engine, but leave the brake disengaged. Or merely sit on your bicycle and relax. The weirdest thing will then happen. You will start to move *uphill*. Whilst there seems to be a pronounced upward slope away from the quartz boulder somehow you will find that you are easing your way up it as if some powerful magical forces are pulling you.

There are many theories about Magnetic Hill. Some, as the name suggests, argue that there is a strong magnetic force in these rocks. Indeed John Hall reports experiments with a compass by the quartz rock, saying it appeared to deflect his readings off the true, thus supporting this assertion. Other theories, of course, centre on the fact that this is right in the midst of the Glen Rushen fairy hotspot, and may therefore be the result of some unseen pixie dust being sprinkled by 'themselves'. Scientifically, the explanation is that this is a remarkable but persuasive optical illusion. If you study the contours on the map they actually descend to the south and east, whereas your eyes certainly tell you that the road ahead is clearly rising. It is a wonderful illusion made all the more dramatic by the way it happens to be positioned in a hotspot for so much supernatural lore.

Lure of the Fairies: Colby Glen (SC 231 708)

Following the A27 south and west from Magnetic Hill you soon arrive in the delightful village of Colby, which has its own glen and some fine views towards the coast. It is also where the fairies were once very active in their desire to lure people deep into their own heartland!

One woman reported being lost on the moors around Colby, and all sense of time and space seeming to disappear. Despite seeing the light of a farmhouse ahead and trying to reach it she felt herself being lured away by the power of the fairies and had to fight to stop herself from being 'took'.

John Hall found another case from 1896. In this story a man walking out on a brilliant night that was rich with stars claimed that he suddenly found himself totally disorientated and on a part of the moors where he was not expecting to be. He also witnessed 'an exhibition' of strange beings and activities that were being played out in some magnificent spectacle in front of his eyes.

Curiously this belief that one can be 'took' by other beings whilst in an altered state of consciousness and then left confused and disorientated remains in claims of alien abduction. These are not common on Mann because when they do happen fairies inevitably still get the blame. Yet no less a story teller than movie producer Steven Spielberg recognized these links when making a TV mini series on alien abduction in 2002. His tale of women kidnapped by small grey aliens was fictional but deliberately infused with elements from actual cases.

It could easily have been set on the Isle of Man, as its otherwise curious title, *Taken*, amply demonstrates.

Even well into modern times there has been a subtle fear around these parts of 'being took', as it is phrased, and children especially were wary of going out at night. According to folklorist Margaret Killip, who collected local stories in the 1960s, even then it was still not strange to say goodbye to a guest with the words, 'Mind you don't get took.' She claims that Manx people felt that the power of Themselves had returned to new heights after decades of repression. This resurgence occurred because of the severe blackout restrictions imposed during the Second World War. Artificial lighting that had made even rural areas so much brighter at night was snuffed out for several years, allowing Themselves to sneak back from their hiding places. Even during the 1960s the risk of abduction was considered stronger than it had been in many decades and, either with real cause or merely through superstition, old fears returned in such parts.

Fairy Hill: Port Erin (SC 195 690)

As its name implies, Port Erin on the south-west of the Island was once the place to board a boat for Ireland. It is still a pretty little village, with a wonderfully protected bay that attracts some fine weather. It is also the end of the line for the steam railway route from Douglas. To get there from Colby by road is also simple. Turn right onto the A7 and proceed west then south through Ballagawne.

Whilst the village itself is worth a look, it is the landscape that surrounds it that is filled with mystery. Much of this is due to Cronk Howe Mooar (SC 205 697), just to the right of the A7 before you enter Port Erin and outside the settlements of Ballachurn and Ballafesson.

This is a small motte, or constructed earth mound, built atop a natural hill and probably marking a Viking fort now destroyed. But again it is an area where earlier Celtic lore predates the traces of such later fortifications. The better-known name for the place is thus significant 'Cronk ny Ferrishyn' (Mx. Gaelic, Hill of the Fairies).

As the name suggests, this is said to be another secret home for Themselves – in fact no less a personage than the fairy king was said to have a palace inside this hillock, which explains why the fear of being 'took' has remained so strong in this vicinity. One is, in effect, trespassing in fairyland.

A Victorian folklorist, Dr Farrell reported of this hill that 'during the summer nights and in the harvest time the elfin throng can be seen – and have been seen hundreds of times – sporting in this glen'. His account, based on descriptions from witnesses, will certainly sound familiar. The fairies, seen glittering in the moonlight, 'vanish with the first ray of sun' but they can often be heard, even when unseen. Fairy Hill is said to be alive 'with a noise resembling a swarm of bees or flies'.

As we have seen, humming hills are commonplace in areas where fairy lore is strong. Moreover the noise of a UFO, when reported as a glowing mass in the sky, is frequently reported by witnesses to resemble that of the buzzing of bees. The connection seems to be much more than coincidental.

South of Port Erin is another fairy settlement, the Meayll Hill Circle (SC 189 678), a megalithic burial site at least 4,000 years old. Human bones have been found here, showing that it was the location of ritual ceremonies far into the past. It is also the source of many modern reports of strange noises, from buzzing sounds to marching of an invisible fairy parade, or the noise of unseen horses of the fairy hunt. Strange lights have also been reported twinkling on the hill at night.

Forces of the Deep: The Sound (SC 172 666)

From the eastern side of Port Erin the A31 climbs and then descends steeply to the south and west, winding narrowly along the 3 or 4 miles (5–6.5 km) of rugged cliffscape towards the tip of the island. It is a spectacular road with some impressive scenery, ending in the wild beauty that is the Sound, where there is a narrow,yet treacheous, stretch of water seperating the mainland from the Calf.

The Calf of Man is a separate island 1 mile (1.5 km) across in both directions dominated by cliffs and intermittently occupied for centuries by those keen to get away from it all. For that reason it has attracted hermits and the religiously minded, as well as observers of nature. Today it is a spectacular habitat for seabirds.

From the Sound (where there is a café and visitor centre with a superb vista), you can walk cautiously down the slopes towards the cliff edge. Here you can see the power of the sea as it crashes against the rocks below. Apart from the seabirds there are also seals, and the many jagged rocks bring home the reason for the memorials you will find dotted on the slopes, commemorating some of the vessels that have come to grief over the centuries.

As you might expect, with its powerful demonstration of the force of nature in the raw, the Sound also has an association with the supernatural. Its proximity to the Meayll Hill circle (only a mile north) further shows that this has long been an area where mankind has felt able to commune with deeper forces. A Scottish folklorist called Campbell who visited the Island in 1860 collected a report from a farm near the Sound. This is the area where sightings of the *glashtin* were at their peak. These blond, blue-eyed human-like entities lived in the wilds and only visited remote farms such as this one in the dead of night. They were amorous folk and sought the attention of any young women who lived in the vicinity.

In this case, a woman was kidnapped by a *glashtin* when she was out in the fields and held captive as he fled towards the Sound. Overcome with great tiredness (the *glashtin* tend to sleep when the sun is up), he lay down holding her tightly by the dress. But she escaped by cutting herself out of her garment, leaving the creature holding only a fistful of cloth.

In UFO lore there are two main types of alien commonly involved in abduction: one is small and akin to the elves or fairies; the other is frequently described by witnesses as tall, human-like, with blond hair and blue eyes. Indeed this type of entity has been given the name 'Nordic' by Ufologists.

Of course, true Nordics are of Viking stock and real Vikings once did raid this part of the Isle of Man and were known to abduct young women. Consequently some historians wonder if these *glashtin* tales from around the Sound are actual folk memories handed down across the generations which recall real events that once occurred here but have been transformed in legend into some sort of supernatural occurrence.

How relevant any of this might be in UFO terms is hard to know. But it is worth a momentary speculation. Do modern fears of kidnap by aliens, which are now so widely reported, awaken some kind of subconscious recall in the minds of people, particularly those of European descent whose ancestors may have suffered actual Viking raids? It would indeed be strange if tales of alien abductions reflect not a technology from space or the future but the memory of raiders from a distant past.

A curious and perhaps relevant case was reported to me by a farmer who in the early 1970s lived west of Port St Mary (SC 215 675).

He woke in the night to see a figure that, at first, he thought was a burglar standing in the gloom of his cottage. It soon became apparent, however, that it was not a real person but the apparition of someone dressed in a very strange manner. The man had an incredible beard, matted and grey and sprouting out of his face as if it were alive. He wore what looked like dirty and extremely frayed animal skins but with a metal plate and sturdy helmet, like a flat skullcap. In one hand he carried a sack and in the other a sword, which he was waving about, apparently pointing through the wall as if motioning towards a particular direction. After a few seconds, the image simply disappeared. The farmer was thereafter convinced that it was the ghost of a Viking raider.

The man also felt that the figure was trying to direct him towards something important by pointing his sword out towards the coast. The farmer never knew what this was, although he came to the conclusion that it might be treasure or even a buried longboat. Nothing like that is known to exist in this immediate area and the matter was dropped in slight embarrassment, without that possibility being explored, especially as the farmer had no proof of his story. Viking ship burials are certainly not unknown on Mann. However, I doubt that archaeologists would mount an expensive investigation on the basis of such a bizarre tale.

There is an old fort, probably of Celtic origin, not far away, known as Burroo Ned (SC 177 665), so there was once military activity locally.

Incidentally, the rocks at nearby Spanish Head (SC 180 659) are reputedly the haunt of the *ben varrey*, mermaids who issue warning messages to sailors who might face danger in these hostile waters. They are said to have risen from the deep amidst a fleet of fishing vessels and howled into the night, 'Make shore!', giving but a few minutes' warning of the arrival of treacherous seas driven by the winds roaring in off the Irish Sea.

Sightings of mermaids from the cliffs here even in modern times are not unknown. However, there are two possible explanations. Seals often play on the rocks below and from a distance can seem mysterious, especially when mist covers the area, as it frequently does. It is also not unheard of for dolphins to frolic in these waters and they can seem particularly mermaid-like.

Stranger on the Shore: Cregneash (SC 188 673)

Heading back eastwards from the Sound one must take the only road that heads inland (the A31), but it is worth stopping off en route at Cregneash, a village that rises Brigadoon-like as you round a sharp curve in the road. A little further up the hill is a useful car park (which is also visited by service buses from around the island). From here you can walk down the short distance into the village. Cregneash is a living museum, in which village life has been preserved much as it would have been in the time before tourism.

The popular movie *Waking Ned*, set in a quaint Irish village, was partly filmed here and it is easy to see why it has been used in other productions. It conveys a sense of having entered a time-warp to experience a long-gone rural lifestyle. Yet, in rather weird contrast, on the hill to the south-east something looms into view as you continue on the A31 that has a more futuristic look; indeed it resembles nothing quite so much as a giant spacecraft that has landed on the ridge! In fact it is a marine communications centre of intriguing design, but one that visitors are likely to wish to photograph to try and fool their friends back home that whilst on the Isle of Man they had their own close encounter!

The coast 1 mile (1.5 km) south of here between Black Head and Perwick Bay is riven with cliffs, headlands and caves that were once the home to smugglers. John Hall thinks this may be why it has a tradition of sea monster – perhaps a beast conjured up by these crooks to ward off prying eyes. It is said to be a *cabyll-ushtey*, part *buggane* and part horse. Jet black in colour. It rose from the sea and inhabited a cave in Black Head. It was even seen walking the shores. Sailors passing this way thought that the only way to placate it was to toss rum overboard!

Indeed the connection with piracy is reinforced by other legends about the creek that leads into Black Head. A notorious pirate was reputed to have stored his treasure in a cave here, the entrance to which is under water except. A curse was placed upon it so that anyone who dared venture inside would die a terrible death from a plague that was reputedly locked inside. The crashing waves made a noise in the hollow that was likened to a bellowing *buggane*, so one can take one's pick of the evils to be found around Black Head, although the chances are that all were merely rumours spread by smugglers.

To this it seems we can now add a new high-tech terror, for in 1978 I was told by a man called Fred Quayle of something he had encountered on the rocks at Perwick Bay. He said that as he was collecting seaweed, he saw a strange figure stooped over a small rocky outcrop, apparently unaware of his presence. Curious to know who might be out there just after dawn, Fred went closer to investigate.

He discovered that the figure was small, perhaps 3 feet 6 inches (1 m) tall, and wearing what looked like a diver's grey wetsuit. On his chest was a belt with a square box with buttons that the figure kept pressing. Turning around the strange being became aware of

Fred and gazed at him almost as if he had never seen a human being before. Without speaking he opened the box on his chest and took out a tiny piece of rock with a greenish gold-flecked coating. He handed it to Fred who, with some trepidation, took it. The entity then pressed another button on the box on his belt and seemed to vanish into thin air.

Fred abandoned his search for seaweed and went home to Port St Mary to investigate the little rock, which did not seem particularly unusual. Needless to say when he told me this peculiar tale I wanted to see it, but this was not possible. He had placed it on his mantelpiece, and later that day when he next looked for it, it had disappeared, just as completely as the small being in the wetsuit.

Although Fred saw no UFO and there are no other reasons to connect this story with alien activity, it shares features with alien contact cases where the origin of similar little entities is certainly believed by the witness to be from outer space. In others, witnesses have claimed to be given equally pointless gifts, including one which was believed to be a diamond, but which proved to be just a piece of quartz.

It is also known that fairies often handed over small gifts to humans whom they had befriended, usually small items of food. And, indeed, in one modern UFO encounter from the USA a farmer was given some very odd-looking pancakes. When tasted, the texture resembled cardboard and when another was studied in a laboratory it was found to be a rather inedible concoction of completely terrestrial ingredients.

So from fairies to aliens the trend of handing over useless and mundane gifts seems to continue.

Ghosts and Ghoulies: Castletown (SC 265 655)

The A31 skirts Port St Mary to the north and at SC 216 687 joins with the A5 coming in from Port Erin. Head east along this for another 2 or 3 miles (3–4.5 km) and you will reach Castletown which, as its name suggests, has a very imposing castle and was also the original capital of Mann. Indeed Douglas did not replace it until the 1860s.

Between Port St Mary and Castletown you cross the Bay ny Carrickey and a stretch of coast known as Black Rocks. This again has associations with smugglers and is said to be home to a frightening sea monster. A witness who saw it was a man returning home near Strandhall around the year 1800. The creature was a huge black thing that rose out of the water and lumbered across the road onto land directly in front of him, heading northwards towards Colby. Again it is hard to know whether this tale was merely spread by the local smugglers or whether it has any substance.

On the road at SC 208 683 is a single, large standing stone believed to be about 3,500 years old, known as the Giant's Quoiting Stone.

Half a mile (800 m) south-east of Strandhall is the interesting archaeological site of Chapel Hill (SC 246 681), overlooking the sea at Balladoole, which contains evidence of its use in three different eras. The oldest is a hill fort of Celtic origin which once must have offered a fine view of the sea to the south and west of Castletown. Later on, a Christain Keeill was erected there.In the late 800s the Vikings realized the importance of the location by making it the spot for a prestigious burial. A Viking chief, along with his 35-foot (10-m) longship and armoury, was buried here and the outline of that fine vessel is still visible and even though the wood has long since rotted away the iron rivets and other artefacts can be seen in the Manx Museum.

The A5 now heads south-west the final mile (1.5 km) into Castletown. Being the former capital, it has more than its fair share of old buildings, which are largely kept in excellent condition. The proximity of the airport, Ronaldsway just a mile (1.5 km) to the north-east, however, sits a little uncomfortably with this antiquity. Thankfully air traffic is relatively light, so the peace is less disturbed than it could be.

Amongst the treasures to see in Castetown is the Old Grammar School (SC 266 674), which dates back 800 years. There is also the superbly restored Old House of Keys (lower house of the Manx parliament).

Castle Rushen (SC 265 674) is widely considered to be one of the best preserved medieval castles in the British Isles. It has a remarkable history, built by the Vikings and later home to the English Lords of Mann.

During the English Civil War, Castle Rushen had a unique role to play when the Islanders, loyal to King Charles, stood against Cromwell's forces until he sent an invading army to force the surrender of the castle and thereby all of Mann. Historical re-creations of events such as this often take place in the atmospheric setting of this imposing building.

In the decade following the temporary ending of the monarchy and whilst Cromwell served as Lord Protector of both Mann and its parent kingdoms there was much talk of the supernatural. We have seen how this period of British history affected Peel Castle (see Chapter 5).

Legends tell how the Celts fought a battle in Castletown with the original fairy inhabitants and drove them from their home near the castle further north and inland towards Rushen Abbey and into the realms where they still hold sway around Glen Rushen. But in revenge the *ben varrey* reputedly sealed off the Island from outside visitors by patrolling the coast so as to prevent the new inhabitants from successfully trading with other lands.

Reinforced by the lack of shipping after the Civil War the mer-people returned in numbers to the coast around Castletown in the 1650s, there were numerous sightings. Belief grew strong that their home was an underwater city now under the waves off Langness, a bleak cape on the east of Castletown Bay. Its lights were seen from time to time by passing fishing boats.

But most remarkable is a story, dating from 1676, soon after the Restoration of the monarchy, when the Island had begun to return to normality. Using a form of primitive submersible, a brave treasure hunter descended in a glass case filled with air slung by ropes over the side of a ship. He was looking for the wreckage of vessels sunk off Langness, but claimed to have found the mermaid city instead. According to reports he descended much further than he was expected to, seeming to go beyond the sea floor, which is relatively close to the surface at this point. He was hauled up in a terrible state after the rope had run down to its full length – his oxygen supplies no doubt close to exhaustion after such a protracted underwater excursion.

When he was able to talk, he expressed huge disappointment that his companions had brought him to the surface when he was having such a fantastic experience. He said that he had dropped below the sea bed to enter a world filled with sunlight. There were pebbled roads, multi-coloured rocks and houses built out of pearly shells. Inside these all manner of jewels and precious stones abounded. The houses were occupied by the *ben varrey* and their male spouses, who stared in a mixture of awe and horror at this man in a glass case invading their kingdom.

In those days, of course, the effects of oxygen starvation to the brain (anoxia) were not well understood and the fact that a sense of spiritual reverie and hallucinations can result was yet to be appreciated. Today some scientists believe that similar conditions (lack of oxygen to the brain following a traumatic accident or heart attack) can result in visions of heavenly places and bright lights. These so called near-death experiences often lead to the person returning to health with an absolute certainty that they have visited the afterlife. Whilst anoxia cannot account for all of these reported cases (in some instances the oxygen flow to the brain was measured and remained intact), it is certainly known that anoxia can be the trigger for some such experiences.

So did this unfortunate submariner almost suffocate as he hovered amidst the ocean depths for longer than anticipated? Did he then have a vision akin to a near-death experience that was based on local beliefs about the mermaid city off Langness? It certainly seems possible, especially as the reports claim that, being unable to return to this wondrous city, which he dearly wanted to do, the seaman lost all concern for life and passed away soon afterwards. High-altitude mountain climbers and balloonists who exceed safety thresholds can suffer similar effects.

Even today Castle Rushen retains its links with the supernatural. Given its history this is unsurprising. It has long been known that prisons are a breeding ground for apparitions, as if the enormous emotions that surround these places somehow leave their mark upon the ether. Apparitions are in fact much more like a TV replay than a face-to-face encounter with a ghost, suggesting that perhaps the emotional trauma somehow imprints itself onto the atmosphere like an action replay that is run from time to time for a suitably perceptive audience.

This possibility is supported by the number of reports of what appears to be the same apparition in Castle Rushen over a period lasting 200 years. Waldron first noted this in the mid-1700s, when there were stories circulating among soldiers guarding the castle in the wake of the Restoration and prisoners who were incarcerated because they were unable to pay their debts. These stories tell of a woman dressed in black standing forlornly by the tower. This was where condemned prisoners were held during the 17th, including a woman who was executed after being convicted of murdering her own child.

One report, which came directly to Waldron, convinced him because he knew the witness to be a well-regarded citizen of Castletown. The man was hurrying to shelter from a sudden storm when he saw a woman by the castle gate, unprotected from the elements yet evidently uncaring. As he walked towards her to check whether she needed help she stepped backwards and disappeared through a locked door.

When I regularly visited Mann in the 1960s it was well known that visitors to the castle had from time to time reported similar sightings, always of a woman and usually somewhere near the keep. In 1937 one of the guides at the castle saw a woman pass by him and move into a room that was once the dungeon, but had been since opened to visitors. He took it to be an ordinary tourist until moments later a man came and asked if he had seen his wife. Assuming that she was the woman he had just seen, the guide searched the dungeon for her. But the room was deserted, although nobody could have left without passing the guide. The man's wife turned up a few minutes later on top of the castle, admiring the spectacular views. She had been there all the time.

The British ghost hunter Andrew Green also came across a sighting from August 1960 in which four men passing by the castle late at night saw a woman in black standing on the tower above the keep. The castle was locked, and the next day, when they reported the matter, it was confirmed that nobody had been inside at the time. The men agreed to sign sworn statements to confirm that they were telling the truth.

There is much to see and enjoy in Castletown amidst this gaggle of strange tales, so this town is probably an appropriate place to end our tour of the mysterious Isle of Man. Douglas is a straight ride from here-only some 8 miles (13 km) along the A5, past the airport and Ballasalla. You can also take the alternative route, the A25, if you want some variety. Join it by turning sharp right at the railway bridge near Ballachrine (SC 299 711). However, the direct way will take you through Santon again and, of course, over Fairy Bridge. If you go that way, then do not forget to say thank you to the little people for allowing you to visit their homeland. And perhaps you can join in the new tradition by leaving a note tied to the branches above the bridge, saying not goodbye to the Isle of Man, but merely 'Until the next time'. Because I suspect that if you are anything like me, one trip to this Island will never be enough. You will want to return again and again.

Appendix A
Some Manx Words

Given its nature it might be useful to have some idea of the Manx language, a mixture of Gaelic and Norse with a smattering of English, to understand the derivations of place names and other words.

The language often seems hard to decipher, with a variety of spellings for the same word. There is also debate over the derivation of some terms. For instance, Manx for fairies is *ferrishyn*. Whilst some commentators think this is an old word and may come from the same Celtic root as the English 'fairy', evidence suggests that it is a relatively modern term based upon the English word. Recall that in Mann they have long tended not to refer to Themselves as 'fairies'.

Balla: farm, as in numerous Manx place names
Beg: little
Ben: woman
Cabbal: chapel
Caillagh: old woman
Chibbyr: well
Cronk: hill
Doo (or dhoo): black
Dooinney: man
Glion: glen

Gob:	mouth or estuary
Keeill:	old church
Laa:	day (*Laa mie*, good day, would be a fine thing to say to the fairies at Ballaglonney Bridge)
Lag:	hollow
Lheeanee:	meadow
Mooar:	great or large
Moddey:	dog
Marrey:	sea
Oie:	night
Spooyt:	waterfall (literally, spout)
Ushtey:	water
Y:	the (also *ny* 'of the')

Appendix B
Manx Customs

Many of the customs of the Island are rooted in the distant past and reflect the belief that the fairy folk are the original occupants of Mann. Sometimes they pass on part of their magical powers to those they favour and this manifests as the gift of second sight. The view that Manx people are more blessed with what we might otherwise call extrasensory perception (ESP) has long been prevalent and it is widely assumed that it is a gift from Themselves, offered to humans only if they are treated favourably in return.

Those who do respect the fairies can be given second sight of such power that it passes from generation to generation. The *tramman* (elder) or fairy tree might be a mark of this. Those who wished to curry favour with Themselves often planted such a tree outside their house and left it exclusively for fairy use. It attracted these beings to the homestead and, it was hoped, they would provide protection or good fortune to its owners. This tree was never to be removed, for to do so courted disaster. As a result you can still find such trees close by the doorways of old Manx properties.

Second sight, if it was granted, was recognized by families in three ways: the person so blessed could see the 'corpse light' – the funeral processions, and the fairy host. The first was the most obvious indicator that second sight had been granted. When a person was lying on their death bed, those possessing such a gift could see a pale misty light rise from the body at the moment of passing. It was believed to be the soul migrating from the physical realm. Mediums still claim to have such an ability, but once upon a time it was believed far more widespread, especially on Mann.

Seeing the funeral procession was a more bizarre phenomenon. The person with second sight was said to be able to see a preview of the actual funeral march a few days in advance. So to see, or merely hear, such a procession was regarded as a good omen personally (you were blessed with second sight) but rather less good for someone that you knew, for they would shortly be passing on.

Once second sight was suspected, because of experiences like these, there was a way to test the extent of its power. A visit to a fairy stronghold, such as Fairy Hill near Port Erin, in the dead of night, could either provide the opportunity to see the fairy host when others would see nothing, or afford the chance to see a procession of the dead, a sort of action replay, perhaps of a ritual performed in ancient times atop this hill. One might observe, as if it were occurring all over again, the ceremony or human sacrifice once carried out to sanctify this spot.

People considered to have second sight through such experiences were listened to by others in the village and greatly respected as a conduit through which the knowledge was transmitted. The medium in this sense was not so much a person who carried messages from the afterlife (as is believed today) but someone favoured by the denizens of fairyland.

Even for those who did not possess second sight, many rituals and precautionary activities existed. Being so closely in tune with the supernatural, many of these rituals or customs are still observed today.

For instance, on 6th January, the 12th day of Christmas, it is still widely considered (even on the British mainland) that certain things must be done without delay. It is considered bad luck to leave your Christmas decorations up beyond that date. On Mann there have been even stronger traditions associated with this date, the oddest of which is the so-called 'cutting off the fiddler's head'. The fiddler, who was regarded as a local wise man, was invited to play and then place his head on the lap of one of the unmarried young women in the community. The names of eligible bachelors would be read out and the fiddler responded to each one as his instinct told him. If his second sight revealed the best match to be made by this woman then it was regarded as almost a binding obligation.

The Irish saint, Bridget is held in special reverence on the Island – note the settlements named after her, such as Kirk Bride and St Bridget's Chapel at The Nunnery, near Douglas. On 1 February, her feast day, it was regarded as good fortune to invite Bridget into the home by placing rushes on the doorstep. Some families went further still and dressed a sheaf of oats in a woman's dress to represent St Bridget, hoping that this would make her feel welcome.

St Patrick's Day (17th March) was a very important date, given the place that this saint had in the history of Mann. Coinciding with the birth of spring, it was also regarded as the perfect day to plan for the summer to come, sowing was carried out in hope of reaping a good harvest.

By 25th April thoughts were turning towards the supernatural forces that would soon be awakened in the landscape once Themselves became active after their winter hibernation. This date is also the feast of St Maughold, was when the forces of the underworld began to stir. It was believed that in the two hours either side of midnight one could see the spirits of the dead dancing in graveyards.

May was the month when Themselves began to reassert their liberty and for the next few months would be a threat to any humans who did not take great care or show them due respect. There were many things that could be done around May Eve and May Day. Primroses were strewn over doorsteps to keep out evil *bugganes,* while a cross made by tying two rowan (mountain ash) twigs together to make a *crosh cuirn* was placed in the barn to protect the animals. Fires were lit on hillsides and horns were blown loudly to scare off any unwanted visitors.

Some of these traditions have lived on, even on the mainland, although their origin is often dressed up as a May Day parade in which young girls pay homage to the elemental forces and gifts of flowers are laid out at well sites. Their supernatural genesis is mostly lost these days in what appears to be merely celebrations to welcome the coming of summer; but they owe much to a fear that if precautions are not taken in a ritualistic manner then the supernatural entities in our midst will make us pay.

Midsummer is now regarded as the night of 24th/25th June, although it is worth remembering that this is a relatively recent placement; the original Midsummer was 4th/5th July. The date was literally moved forward when the modern calendar was introduced. Such was the need to readjust dates that what was then 24th June became 5th July by the new reckoning. As a consequence, both these dates are associated with Midsummer rituals.

Tynwald, the annual outdoor ceremony where the parliamentary Acts are read out, was always conducted around Midsummer's Day and remains fixed on 5th July (unless it happens to fall on a Saturday or Sunday when it is moved to a weekday).

Another interesting Manx tradition regarding Midsummer's Eve is that on this very night the fairies are believed to grant humans the power to leave their bodies and float through the ether. In our dreams we can thus experience what appear to be out-of-body states and drift over the landscape or visit our loved ones in supernatural form without them being aware what we are doing.

For weeks after Midsummer, the legions of Themselves ruled the roost once more and travellers at night were always warned to be careful or else they might be 'took'. This was especially true on 1st August, *Laa Lunys*.

On *Laa Lunys* (connected with the Celtic god Lug, said to have been brought up at the court of Manannan), it was the practice to visit the highest hill in the locality or to attend a holy well, where offerings were made in a variety of forms, ranging from dropping coins into the water to placing small presents on branches of overhanging trees. The aim was to ask the powers- that-be to cure any illnesses that may have developed or grant small favours to ease the burden of life.

The Church was especially offended by this old tradition and sought to stamp it out, but ironically it is perhaps the most widespread and persistent of all such beliefs even now. Wishing wells are, of course, commonplace across the UK and usually no more than a gimmick, but they are based on this once very real ritual. As we have seen, the idea of offering small presents, or leaving messages and asking for favours from Themselves, has recently seen a considerable revival at Ballaglonney Bridge.

Even for those with no knowledge of the old ways or belief in fairies, there is one date in the calendar that we all recognize – Hallowe'en, called *Hop tu Naa* in the Isle of Man, the night when all manner of supernatural forces awaken.

Of course, we have turned this (like all the other ritual dates) into something of a holiday, but it was once a very real night of fear for those living on Mann. Of course, whilst we celebrate this night as 31 October, like Midsummer it was originally found later in the calendar (11 November in fact). All Hallow's Eve (known as *Oie Houiney* in Manx) was kept as 11 November on the Island for rather longer than elsewhere. In order to placate Themselves, who would be feasting and dancing that night in preparation for the winding down of their activities over winter, it was customary to do something to please them. Most common was to leave the remains of one's supper un-cleared and put out crocks of fresh water for them.

This night was also long regarded as the turning of the year and a time for prediction.

One of the strangest customs was the baking of Dumb Cake (*soddag valloo*), a non-too tasty concoction of eggshells, flour and soot, made by the young women of the household, who baked it over the hot turf ashes and ate it in silence while walking backwards towards bed. The expected outcome was that the young women would each dream of their future husband.

Only pale shadows of such ancient traditions now remain. It is still unusually common for people to greet the stroke of midnight that welcomes the New Year with a spoken magical incantation that varies but is often some sort of lucky charm (the words 'white rabbits' spoken three times is an example). These must be the words that break the silence after the clock strikes midnight if they are to be successful in invoking the powers of the supernatural realm to grant you good fortune over the coming weeks. That even in these days of mobile phones and space travel we take such actions seriously is a powerful testament to the forces at work here. Millions of otherwise rational people are willing to do it in the privacy of their own home, which shows that we are not so far removed from the seemingly bizarre ideas and activities that were once so widespread.

Appendix C
Transport on the Isle of Man

The tours described in this book have been created on the assumption that you will be driving around the Isle of Man. This is certainly the ideal way to see the most things in the shortest time and driving your own car on the Island is not difficult, especially out of high season when many of the roads are quiet. However, the extraordinary transport system on Mann is a delight in itself and the network is very well designed.

There are three 'heritage' railways: the Isle of Man Steam Railway, the Manx Electric Railway and the Snaefell Mountain Railway (which runs from Laxey MER Station).Their use will allow access to many of the sites in this text without recourse to a motor car at all – although a little walking is likely to be involved, of course. Check up to date timetables for routes and times to use public transport to its best advantage.

The Isle of Man Steam Railway route is the last of three original lines, the others having sadly closed. It was built in 1874 as a narrow-gauge track but using relatively large locomotives and stock. The surviving route operates from Douglas to Port Erin, covering almost 20 miles (32 km) and serving the south. There are stations en route at Port Soderick, Santon, Ballasalla, Ronaldsway, Castletown, Ballabeg, Colby, Level and Port St Mary. The journey takes about an hour. At the superb Victorian station, near the quay at Douglas, the old-world charm of the buffet and ticket office adds to the atmosphere as you await your departure. At the

Port Erin terminus there is a small museum about the Island's steam railway heritage.

The Manx Electric Railway is an 18-mile-long (29 km) spectacular system that runs northwards along the coast between Douglas, Laxey and Ramsey. Opened in 1899 it is operated by old-style trams not unlike the cable cars in San Francisco but using overhead power via a trolley pole. It runs along conventional railway tracks with sleepers for much of the way. These operate on a separate alignment that is largely adjacent to the main roads and, like the steam railway, serve as both a proper transport artery and an amazing tourist attraction.

The line starts on the northern end of Douglas sea front (near Derby Castle) and major stations are at Groudle, Baldrine, South Cape, Laxey, Dhoon, Ballaglass, Ballajora and with the other terminus in central Ramsey. The journey from Douglas to Laxey takes about 30 minutes and from Laxey to Ramsey another 45 minutes.

The Snaefell Mountain Railway was opened in 1895 and like the Manx Electric Railway, of which this is effectively a branch, uses old-style electric trams. It starts at the interchange station with the Manx Electric Railway at Laxey and then climbs the 7 miles (11 km) up to the summit of Snaefell at 2,036 feet (620 m). There is one intermediary station at The Bungalow interchanging with the main road and TT route part way up the mountain.

This line is very weather-dependent as the ascent is gruelling and the summit of Snaefell is best appreciated in good conditions. Generally the trains run between May and September. The climb takes about 30 minutes.

A good way to connect between the Sea Terminal in Douglas Bay and the Electric Railway is by horse tram. This is a unique transport system that really goes backover 100 years. The service only runs during the summer months (early May to late September). The terminus is at Derby Castle near where the Manx Electric Railway commences.

Of course, these romantic forms of transport, important as they are to the Manx communication network, are supplemented by more comfortable, modern vehicles. There is an extensive network of road buses – mostly of very up-to-date specifications that include both single and double decker that reach all parts of the Island – including those locations in this book that are not served by rail, such as Peel, Glen Maye and St John's.

Visitors will find that 'rover' tickets allow unlimited travel on most buses, trains and trams.

Being such a relatively small island, it is also possible to utterly forsake mechanical transportation and either cycle or walk wherever you want to go. The committed walker or cyclist could certainly cover much of the Island during a two week stay, probably with time to spare. It is easy to take cycles on the ferries and there are plenty of hire shops if you choose not to do so. Special cycle routes cover the Island making it simple to tour this way in good safety.

Walkers are even better catered for with an excellent series of hill and coastal trails designed to bring some spectacular views.

The most ambitious walking trail is the Raad ny Foillan (Road of the Gull) circling the entire coastline. It runs for 90 miles (145 km) so you need to be fit! Another is the 28-mile (45 km) Millennium Way from Ramsey to Castletown. But the easiest and within the reach of any hiker is the relatively flat Heritage Trail. This is 10 miles (16 km) long and covers the course of the closed steam railway between Quarterbridge, on the TT course just outside Douglas, all the way to Peel.

Timetables, tickets and leaflets are all available at the Welcome Centre at the Sea Terminal.

Bibliography

The following publications all provide information of relevance to the supernatural background of the Isle of Man or will give more details about the general topics featured in this text. Many of the texts that refer specifically to the Island are very old and not now in publication; although a few have been reprinted in modern facsimile format. Others are probably only accessible via specialist sources such as the Manx National Heritage Library in Douglas or on-line.

General

Asala, Joanne, Celtic Tales of the Strange, Sterling, New York, 1997
Bord, Janet and Colin, Modern Mysteries of Britain, Grafton, 1987
Broome, Dora, Fairy Tales from the Isle of Man, Penguin, 1951
Cashen, William, Manx Folklore, G. & L. Johnson, 1912
Crellin, A.M., Manx Folklore, Chiollagh, Peel, 1994
Farrell, Dr R., Beyond the Silver Streak in Manxland, John Heywood, Manchester, 1894
Fort, Charles, Lo!, Reprinted, John Brown Publishing, 1996
Gill, Walter, A Manx Scrapbook, Arrowsmith, 1929
Killip, Margaret, The Folklore of the Isle of Man, Batsford, 1975
Manx National Heritage, Ancient and Historic Monuments of the Isle of Man, Manx National Heritage, 1973
Moore, A.W., Folklore of the Isle of Man, Llanerch Press, Felinfach, 1944
Morrison, Sophia, Manx Fairy Tales, Reprinted, Manx Experience, Douglas, 1991 and update by Lily Publications, 2013.

Price, Harry and Lambert, R.S., The Haunting of Cashen's Gap, Metheun, 1936
Train, Joseph, History of the Isle of Man, Quiggin, Douglas 1845
Waldron, George, A Description of the Isle of Man, Reprinted, Manx Society, Douglas, 1864
Wentz, W. Evans, The Fairy Faith in Celtic Countries, OUP, 1911
Young, G.V.C., A Brief History of the Isle of Man, Mansk-Svenska, Peel, 1983

Fairies
Briggs, Katherine, The Fairies in Tradition and Literature, Routledge, 1967
Briggs, Katherine, A Dictionary of Fairies, Allen Lane, 1976
Vallee, Dr Jacques, Passport to Magonia, Spearman, 1967

Creatures
Costello, Peter, The Magic Zoo, Sphere, 1979

UFOs
Halliday, Ron, UFO Scotland, B & W, Edinburgh, 1998
Hynek, Dr J. Allen, The UFO Experience, Regnery, Chicago, 1972
Randles, Jenny, Abduction, Hale, 1988
Randles, Jenny, Star Children, Hale, 1994

Hauntings
Green, Andrew, Our Haunted Kingdom, Wolfe, 1973
Hough, Peter, Supernatural Britain, Piatkus, 1994
Randles, Jenny, Time Storms, Piatkus, 2001
Randles, Jenny, Supernatural Pennines, Hale, 2002

Mythology
Meaden, Dr Terence, Goddess of the Stones, Souvenir, 1991

Crop Circles
Randles, Jenny and Paul Fuller, Crop Circles: A Mystery Solved, Hale, 1993

Journals

I warmly commend the researches of paranormal investigator John Hall, whose 1990s work based on walking some of the Manx ghost roads can be found under the title 'Haunted Roads on the Isle of Man' in *The Researcher*, various issues, 1999–2001. The Researcher is a subscription-only journal of the Merseyside Anomalies Research Association, 52 Hawthorne Avenue, Halewood, Liverpool L26 9XD.

Other journals of interest include:

Fortean Times
The Ley Hunter
Northern UFO News

Index